TEN
COMMANDMENTS
FOR THE
ENVIRONMENT

Woodeene Koenig-Bricker has done a great service by drawing together from many sources Pope Benedict's teaching on creation and environmental responsibility, and showing how through diplomatic interventions, pastoral initiatives, social teaching and the engineering of Vatican City itself his papacy is fully engaged in the green revolution.

Drew Christiansen, S.J.
Editor-in-Chief, *America*

The Catholic Church has often been slow to engage on issues—but once engaged, it can be a powerful force. In this volume, the current pope shows not only an understanding of the science behind the environmental problems now overwhelming us, but also a subtle and useful grasp of the way they are rooted in a consumer mentality. That message is neither liberal nor conservative—it is just plain hopeful.

Bill McKibben
Author of *Deep Economy*

Ten Commandments for the Environment is a timely and rich resource of the teaching of the Holy Father and Vatican officials concerning the stewardship of our planet Earth. As the teaching of the Catholic Church on the environment continues to expand, this collection of quotations and theological reflections provides a valuable foundation for further development and vision for the future.

Bishop William S. Skylstad
Diocese of Spokane

The need to care for creation is brought to an explicit Catholic focus in this short but well-written book. With a spotlight on the writings of Pope Benedict XVI, Woodeene Koenig-Bricker shows that the Holy Father is deeply invested in ecological issues. These commandments give a broad blueprint for those who want to integrate the teachings of Catholic faith with current environmental and scientific concerns. Timely, balanced, and informative, *Ten Commandments for the Environment* is an important book for all those who desire a sustainable future.

Ilia Delio, O.S.F.
Professor and Chair of Spirituality Studies
Washington Theological Union, Washington, DC

WOODEENE KOENIG-BRICKER

TEN COMMANDMENTS FOR THE ENVIRONMENT

POPE BENEDICT XVI

Speaks Out for CREATION *and* JUSTICE

ave maria press  notre dame, indiana

Founded in 1865, Ave Maria Press is a ministry of the Indiana Province of Holy Cross.

www.avemariapress.com

ISBN-10 1-59471-211-5   ISBN-13 978-1-59471-211-1

Cover image ©Vatican Pool/Corbis.

Cover and text design by Katherine Robinson Coleman.

Printed and bound in the United States of America.

Library of Congress Cataloging-in-Publication Data

        Benedict XVI, Pope, 1927-
    Ten commandments for the environment : Pope Benedict XVI speaks out for creation and justice / Woodeene Koenig-Bricker.
        p. cm.
    Includes bibliographical references.
    ISBN-13: 978-1-59471-211-1
    ISBN-10: 1-59471-211-5
    1. Human ecology—Religious aspects—Catholic Church. 2. Environmentalism—Religious aspects—Christianity. 3. Catholic Church—Doctrines. I. Koenig-Bricker, Woodeene. II. Title.
    BX1795.H82B46 2009
    261.8'8—dc22

2009

006162

CONTENTS

THE

GREEN

POPE

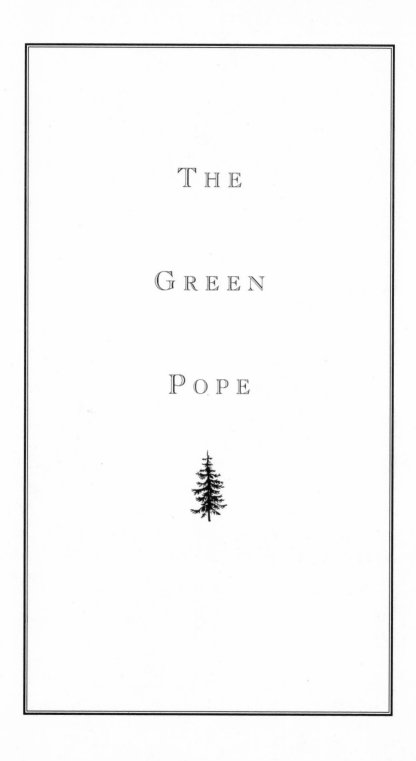

It's tantalizing to imagine the moral force and power of persuasion a green Pope might have on the world," pondered the website World Changing, a global network of secular journalists dedicated to finding solutions to the environmental issues facing the earth, upon the death of Pope John Paul II in 2004.

Few imagined Cardinal Joseph Ratzinger would become that Pope.

When he was elected the two-hundred-sixty-sixth Pope, the world did not anticipate the scholarly German theologian would spend his years making what amounts to virtual campaign speeches on the need for clean water, solar energy, and the reduction of CO_2 emissions. Much to the surprise of fans and foes alike, the man who was once seen as "God's Rottweiler" has quietly, with passionate resolve, spread a message that seems more in keeping with an environmental scientist than a spiritual leader: "Save the planet!"

Perhaps realizing that at his age, he had little time to waste, the Holy Father even spoke about the environment in his homily at the inauguration of his papacy:

> The external deserts in the world are growing, because the internal deserts have become so

vast. Therefore the earth's treasures no longer serve to build God's garden for all to live in, but they have been made to serve the powers of exploitation and destruction. The Church as a whole and all her Pastors, like Christ, must set out to lead people out of the desert, towards the place of life, towards friendship with the Son of God, towards the One who gives us life, and life in abundance.[1]

By August 2006, the Holy Father was already deeply invested in ecological issues, one of the first of which was the September 1 appeal for the protection of creation that all of the churches in Italy planned to celebrate. This nationwide focus on environmental protection was a first for the Church in Italy. During his Angelus address on August 27, the Pope made his first serious call to a commitment to care for creation. He observed that creation is "exposed to serious risks by life choices and lifestyles that can degrade it." In particular, he said, "environmental degradation makes the lives of the poor especially unbearable."

This was just the beginning. In April 2007, the Vatican sponsored a two-day scientific conference for more than seventy scientists, politicians, activists, and church officials on "Climate Change and Development" to underscore the role that religious leaders around the world could play in reminding people that willfully damaging the environment is sinful. In an introductory telegram at the opening of the conference, Benedict expressed the hope that the conference would result in "research and promotion of styles of life and models of production and consumption which are designed for respect of creation and the real exigencies of sustainable progress of peoples, taking account of the universal destination of goods, as has been repeatedly confirmed by the social doctrine of the church."

Later that year, in September 2007, the Pope was in Austria for a three-day visit. The central topic of his homily at the Cathedral of Vienna was about the need to "give the soul its Sunday and the Sunday its soul," but Benedict also reminded listeners:

> At a time when creation seems to be endangered in so many ways through human activity, we should consciously advert to this dimension of Sunday too. Then, for the early Church, the first day increasingly assimilated the traditional meaning of the seventh day, the Sabbath. We participate in God's rest, which embraces all of humanity. Thus we sense on this day something of the freedom and equality of all God's creatures.[2]

The Pope continued to address environmental concerns in 2008. During the summer of 2008, Benedict spent part of his three-week vacation walking through the scenic landscapes in northern Italy, not far from the Austrian border. In the middle of his break, on August 6, he took time to meet and talk with some four hundred priests of the diocese of Bolzano-Bressanone in the local cathedral. There he answered a few of the priests' questions, including one question from Fr. Karl Golser, a professor of moral theology in Bressanone, a well-known eco-theologian, and the director of the Institute for Justice, Peace, and the Preservation of the Creation. Fr. Golser asked the Pope to reflect on ways in which we can increase the sense of responsibility for Creation among our fellow Christians and also increase awareness of the unity of Creation and Redemption. Below we shall examine Benedict's answer; here, however, we simply wish to note that in question-and-answer sessions such as this, which have become customary in Benedict's papacy, the selection of questions is always significant—clearly, environmental issues were on Benedict's mind, and close to his heart.

In December 2008 Pope Benedict named the afore-mentioned Fr. Karl Golser as Bishop of the Bolzano-Bressanone diocese. This selection had personal significance for Benedict, as Bolzano-Bressanone is located in the largely German-speaking Alpine region of northern Italy where the Pope's family on his mother's side has its roots and where Benedict and his family have taken their annual vacation since the late 1960s. As John L. Allen Jr. reported, "With today's appointment, Benedict entrusted this diocese, for which he has deep personal affection, to one of European Catholicism's most outspoken advocates for strong environmental sensitivity."[3]

A Candid Appeal

Benedict has addressed his message in a special way to the youth of the Church. "Before it's too late, we need to make courageous choices that will recreate a strong alliance between man and Earth," the Pope told half a million young Catholics attending a rally near Ancona, on the Adriatic coast, in September 2007. "We need a decisive 'yes' to care for creation and a strong commitment to reverse those trends that risk making a situation of decay irreversible."[4]

In the summer of 2008, the Holy Father traveled to Sydney, Australia, for the twenty-third World Youth Day. Although the prevailing theme of his message was the power of the Holy Spirit, he did not leave his environmental message behind. In his opening remarks, he stated:

> Many young people today lack hope. They are perplexed by the questions that present themselves ever more urgently in a confusing world, and they are often uncertain which way to turn for answers. They see poverty and injustice and they long to find solutions. They are challenged by the arguments of those who deny the existence of God and they wonder how to respond. They see great damage done to the natural environment through human greed and they struggle to find ways to live in greater harmony with nature and with one another.[5]

Thus, with unanticipated candor, Benedict has woven his plea for a renewed commitment to care for the earth in talks to such diverse audiences as the youth of the world, seminarians, scientists, world leaders, and the average Catholic. From private audiences to gatherings of hundreds of thousands at major world events like World Youth Day, Benedict has used his moral force and power of persuasion to bring one of the most critical issues facing the world out of the realm of politicians and scientists into the moral lives of everyday Christians.

A Message Rooted in Tradition

Benedict's message is clear: Being green is as much a moral and religious imperative as it is an environmental concern.

> I believe, therefore, that true and effective measures against the waste and destruction of creation can only be realized and developed,

understood and lived, when creation is considered from the point of view of God; when life is considered on the basis of God and has its major dimensions in responsibility before God; life that one day will be given by God in its fullness and never taken away.[6]

As is fitting in his role as a spiritual leader, Benedict roots his concern not only in science, but also in theology. For him, being green begins and ends with the Creator, who is also our Redeemer:

The Redeemer is the Creator—and if we do not proclaim God in his total grandeur, as Creator and Redeemer, then we also debase Redemption. If God has nothing to do with Creation, when he is present only in some part of history, then how can he encompass our life? How can he bring healing to man in his wholeness and to the world in its totality? That is why a renewal of the doctrine of Creation and a new understanding of the inseparability of Creation and Redemption is of great importance.[7]

Benedict's focus on the theological significance of creation is deeply rooted in the Christian tradition. In 1225, St. Francis of Assisi wrote his famous "Canticle of the Sun" in which he praised all of creation, especially "our sister, mother earth, who sustains and keeps us. And brings forth diverse fruits with grass and flowers bright."[8] Likewise, St. Anthony of Padua (1195–1231) said, "Our thoughts ought instinctively to fly upwards from animals, men, and natural objects to their Creator. If things created are so full of loveliness, how resplendent with beauty must be He who made them! The wisdom of the Worker is apparent in His handiwork."[9] Going back even further, the Psalmist sang, "The earth is the Lord's and all it contains" (Ps 24:1).

Moreover, Benedict is building his current ecological message on the foundation laid by his immediate predecessor, Pope John Paul II. The Polish pontiff opened the trail for the Vatican's ecological concerns, starting with his 1988 encyclical *Sollicutudo Rei Socialis* ("On Social Concern"), which was the first time a Pope had formally addressed ecological matters. His 1990 World Day of Peace statement, "Peace With All of Creation," was the first formal papal document devoted to environmental issues. Under John Paul's papacy, the Vatican became increasingly vocal about ecological and environmental issues. Near the end of his reign, he said eloquently:

> It is necessary, therefore, to stimulate and sustain the "ecological conversion," which over these last decades has made humanity more sensitive when facing the catastrophe toward which it was moving. Man is no longer "minister" of the Creator. However, as an autonomous despot, he is understanding that he must finally stop before the abyss. "Another welcome sign is the growing attention being paid to the 'quality of life' and to 'ecology,' especially in more developed societies, where people's expectations are no longer concentrated so much on problems of survival as on the search for an overall improvement of living conditions" (*Evangelium Vitae*, 27). Therefore, not only is a "physical" ecology at stake, attentive to safeguarding the habitat of different living beings, but also a "human" ecology that will render the life of creatures more dignified, protecting the radical good of life in all its manifestations and preparing an environment for future generations that is closer to the plan of the Creator. [10]

While Benedict builds soundly on John Paul's foundation, one thing that makes his approach somewhat different is the consistency and regularity with which he has emphasized the environmental message. "We must awaken consciences," he has said. "We have to face up to this great challenge and find the ethical capacity to change the situation of the environment for the good."

Practicing What He Preaches

But what really sets Benedict apart in the annals of the Church's teaching on social responsibility in relation to environmental issues is that he is keenly aware that rhetoric alone will not change people's lives. The Pope has therefore opted to lead as much by example as by instruction.

It is obvious that, despite a sea of words, the lifestyles of Catholics do not differ much from those of their neighbors. Catholics consume as much as their fellow citizens. In fact, some of the most Catholic countries like Italy, Mexico, Poland, and France have some of the highest carbon dioxide emissions, a leading cause of global warming. Given that Catholics make up nearly a quarter of the U.S. population and the U.S. tops the list for CO_2 emissions, American Catholics have to be placed on the list as well.

This is where Benedict becomes the "greenest" Pope in history, by putting his words into practice. Most people are shocked to learn that in 2007 the Vatican became the world's first carbon-neutral country, meaning greenhouse gas emissions are offset through renewable energies and carbon credits, beating out Iceland, New Zealand, Norway, and Costa

Rica, who had also been vying for that honor. Although Vatican City is a tiny entity in terms of both size and population, its trailblazing example shows that even a country whose army dresses in sixteenth-century uniforms can effectively enter the twenty-first century with regard to environmental concerns. One of the ways Benedict has accomplished this is through a reforestation project in a Hungarian national park. (One can't help but wonder if replanting part of the Black Forest in Benedict's beloved Germany is on his agenda as well.)

Another place where Benedict has demonstrated practical leadership is in solar energy, replacing the cement roof tiles of the Paul VI auditorium with 2,400 solar panels that convert sunlight into some 300,000 kilowatt-hours of power each year, which is equivalent to the needs of about one hundred families. The cells generate energy to light, heat, and cool the six-thousand-seat hall. When the hall is not in use, any surplus energy will be used by the Vatican power network. The panels are expected to reduce carbon dioxide emissions by about 225 tons and save the equivalent of eighty tons of oil each year.[11] In addition, another solar-panel system will be installed above the Vatican's employee cafeteria, which will provide 60 to 70 percent of that building's power.[12]

But that's not all. Vatican engineer Mauro Villarini says that experts are considering other "green" projects for Vatican City and the papal estate at Castel Gandolfo, including the possibility of installing small windmills as well as treatment plants to break down water-waste products. And on the 740 acres north of Rome at Santa Maria di Galeria, which is used as a transmission center for Vatican Radio, a solar energy system is being considered. Vatican officials say the Vatican plans to have sufficient renewable energy sources to provide 20 percent of its needs by 2020. (For those who worry that the beauty and majesty of St. Peter's might be marred by solar panels or windmills, the Vatican assures that beloved historical landmarks will not be touched.)[13]

Finally, Benedict understands that most people want to live greener, more responsible lives, but they often do not know how or where to begin. Thus, the Vatican has issued, through the Pontifical Council for Justice and Peace, Ten Commandments for the Environment. As Bishop Giampaolo Crepaldi, secretary of the Pontifical Council for Justice and Peace, told Vatican Radio, the "commandments" are an attempt "to explain in ten points the most important aspects of the chapter on the environment in the *Compendium of the Social Doctrine of the Church.*"

These commandments give a broad blueprint for those who want to integrate the teachings of the faith with current environmental and scientific concerns. In the rest of this book, we will take a deeper look at how these commandments fit into the broader framework of Catholic social teaching and Pope Benedict's teaching about environmental issues, as well as examine ways in which each of us, as individuals and as families can, as Benedict has asked, make "our style of life . . . a form of witness" and make our words "express the faith in a credible way as an orientation in our time."

COMMANDMENTS

FOR THE

ENVIRONMENT

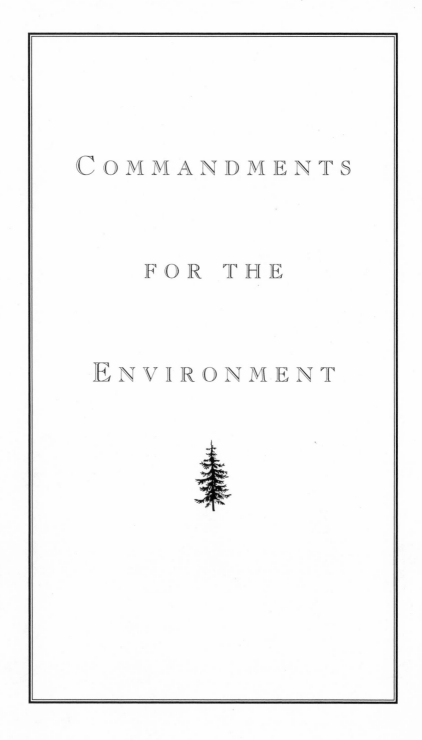

I t might be argued that Catholic social teaching began just before the Ascension. After cooking a breakfast of fish and bread, Jesus was enjoying what was presumably a lovely spring morning with his disciples when he asked Peter a significant question: "Do you love me?" He asked not once, not twice, but three times, responding to Peter's increasing distress by reiterating the command to "Feed my sheep" (Jn 21:15–19).

While those words have been given the metaphorical meaning of providing spiritual nourishment and leadership to Christian followers, there may be a literal meaning contained in them as well. Drawing from and building on the Jewish traditions of caring for the widowed and orphans, Catholic teaching has always given precedence to helping the less fortunate, the so-called "preferential option for the poor." Rooted in the biblical concept of justice, this teaching is not limited to those who lack economic goods, but extends to all who are deprived or vulnerable, calling on both individuals and social institutions to provide for the common good through an equitable distribution of the world's resources.

Over the past two thousand years, the Church has cared for the less fortunate in many ways, both formally and informally. However, what we understand today as the official principles of Catholic social teaching have developed somewhat more recently, starting only in the late nineteenth century. These principles have been called "the best kept secret of the Catholic faith." As the U.S. Catholic Bishops said in "Sharing Catholic Social Teaching: Challenges and Directions":

> Far too many Catholics are not familiar with the basic content of Catholic social teaching. More fundamentally, many Catholics do not adequately understand that the social teaching of the Church is an essential part of Catholic faith. This poses a serious challenge for all Catholics, since it weakens our capacity to be a Church that is true to the demands of the Gospel. We need to do more to share the social mission and message of our Church.[1]

In order to understand how the very latest development in this teaching—a new focus on ecology and the environment, including the issuing of the Ten Commandments for the Environment—came about, we need to take a brief excursion into the evolution of Catholic teaching on the collective welfare of humanity.

The Story Behind Benedict's Message

Late in the nineteenth century, the Church began to take a long, hard look at issues of social justice on a formal scale. Living conditions for the poor had never been pleasant, but with the Industrial Revolution and the creation of the factory system of manufacturing, harsh working conditions, especially for children, increased. In Europe popular novels like *David Copperfield* by Charles Dickens began to call attention to the plight of the poor in ways never before expressed. Likewise, in America, *Uncle Tom's Cabin* by Harriet Beecher Stowe revealed the appalling conditions of slavery, showing that so-called "good Christians" were enslaving other human beings.

In 1891, Pope Leo XIII entered this volatile environment with the encyclical *Rerum Novarum* ("Of New Things"), focusing on capital and labor, the working class, and the relationship of citizens to government. Then, in 1931, in commemoration of the fortieth anniversary of *Rerum Novarum*, Pope Pius XI issued the encyclical *Quadragesimo Anno* ("In the Fortieth Year"), which expanded on the earlier encyclical and addressed the topic of industrialization as well as capitalism, socialism, and communism. With this encyclical, Catholic social teaching began to emerge as an important aspect of Catholic teaching. This encyclical remained the basis of the doctrine for another thirty years, until 1961, when Pope John XXIII issued *Mater et Magistra* ("Mother and Teacher"), which focused on social progress, relationships between rich and poor nations, and global economic imbalances. Two years later, Pope John further expanded his thoughts in *Pacem in Terris* ("Peace on Earth"), in which he demonstrated the relationship of world peace to the rights and responsibilities of persons.

It was the Second Vatican Council, however, that launched Catholic social teaching fully into the modern era. The conciliar text *Gaudium et Spes*, or the *Pastoral Constitution on the Church and the Modern World*, examined a broad range of social issues and reemphasized the fundamental dignity of every human individual. After the council, Pope Paul VI continued the theme in 1967 with *Populorum Progressio* ("The Development of Peoples"), calling on rich nations to assist poorer ones in the cause of development and peace.

When John Paul II was elected in 1978, he built on and greatly expanded his predecessors' work. In particular, his encyclical *Laborem Exercens* ("On Human Work") examined the dignity of human labor, laying the foundation for increased ecological concerns by stating:

> The word of God's revelation is profoundly marked by the fundamental truth that *man*, created in the image of God, *shares by his work in the activity of the Creator* and that, within the limits of his own human capabilities, man in a sense continues to develop that activity, and perfects it as he advances further and further in the discovery of the resources and values contained in the whole of Creation. . . . The knowledge that by means of work man shares in the work of Creation constitutes the most profound *motive* for undertaking it in various sectors. (*Laborem Exercens*, 25)

The environmental message was developed tremendously with John Paul's 1988 encyclical *Sollicitudo Rei Socialis*, the first encyclical that contained a substantive discussion of ecological concerns. It laid the foundation for future examination of these critical issues by connecting ecology with human dignity and environmental protection with personal morality. The Pope wrote:

> We must also mention a greater realization of the limits of available resources, and of the need to respect the integrity and the cycles of nature and to take them into account when planning for development, rather than sacrificing them to certain demagogic ideas about the latter. Today this is called ecological concern. . . .

Nor can the moral character of development exclude respect for the beings which constitute the natural world, which the ancient Greeks— alluding precisely to the order which distinguishes it—called the "cosmos." Such realities also demand respect, by virtue of a threefold consideration which it is useful to reflect upon carefully.

The first consideration is the appropriateness of acquiring a growing awareness of the fact that one cannot use with impunity the different categories of beings, whether living or inanimate— animals, plants, the natural elements—simply as one wishes, according to one's own economic needs. On the contrary, one must take into account the nature of each being and of its mutual connection in an ordered system, which is precisely the cosmos.

The second consideration is based on the realization—which is perhaps more urgent—that natural resources are limited; some are not, as it is said, renewable. Using them as if they were inexhaustible, with absolute dominion, seriously endangers their availability not only for the present generation but above all for generations to come.

The third consideration refers directly to the consequences of a certain type of development on the quality of life in the industrialized zones. We all know that the direct or indirect result of industrialization is, ever more frequently, the pollution of the environment, with serious consequences for the health of the population.

Once again it is evident that development, the planning which governs it, and the way in which resources are used must include respect for moral demands. One of the latter undoubtedly imposes limits on the use of the natural world. The dominion granted to man by the Creator is not an absolute power, nor can one speak of a freedom to "use and misuse," or to dispose of things as one pleases. The limitation imposed from the beginning by the Creator himself and expressed symbolically by the prohibition not to "eat of the fruit of the tree" (cf. Gen 2:16–17) shows clearly enough that, when it comes to the natural world, we are subject not only to biological laws but also to moral ones, which cannot be violated with impunity.

A true concept of development cannot ignore the use of the elements of nature, the renewability of resources and the consequences of haphazard industrialization—three considerations which alert our consciences to the moral dimension of development. (*Sollicitudo Rei Socialis*, 26–34)

This was followed by the 1990 World Day of Peace message, "Peace with All Creation," the first formal Vatican document dealing exclusively with ecological matters. In it, John Paul clearly pointed out:

[World peace] is threatened not only by the arms race, regional conflicts, and continued injustices among peoples and nations, but also by a lack of *due respect for nature*, by the plundering of natural resources and by a progressive decline in the quality of life. The sense of precariousness and insecurity that such a situation engenders is a seedbed for collective selfishness, disregard for others, and dishonesty. . . .

Faced with the widespread destruction of the environment, people everywhere are coming to understand that we cannot continue to use the goods of the earth as we have in the past. The public in general as well as political leaders are concerned about this problem, and experts from a wide range of disciplines are studying its causes. Moreover, a new *ecological awareness* is beginning to emerge which, rather than being downplayed, ought to be encouraged to develop into concrete programs and initiatives.[2]

Near the end of his pontificate, in June 2002, Pope John Paul II issued the Common Declaration on Environmental Ethics with the Ecumenical Patriarch of the Greek Orthodox Church, Bartholomew I. The Declaration expressed their common belief in the goodness of Creation, the dignity of all people, and the idea that moral failure lies at the root of the ecological crises facing the world.

Respect for Creation stems from respect for human life and dignity. It is on the basis of our recognition that the world is created by God that we can discern an objective moral order within which to articulate a code of environmental ethics. In this perspective, Christians and all other believers have a specific role to play in proclaiming moral values and in educating people in *ecological awareness*, which is none other than responsibility towards self, towards others, towards Creation.[3]

A Unified Vision

As we have seen, over the past hundred years the tradition of Catholic social teaching has steadily grown to include a number of documents addressing a wide range of issues. In light of this complexity, in his Post-synodal Apostolic Exhortation "Ecclesia in America," Pope John Paul II noted that "it would be very useful to have a compendium or approved synthesis of Catholic social doctrine . . . which would show the connection between it and the new evangelization." Five years later, in 2004, the *Compendium of the Social Doctrine of the Church* was unveiled; it was issued by the Pontifical Council for Justice and Peace and was dedicated to Pope John Paul II. As the introduction to the document states, the intention of the *Compendium* is:

> to present in a complete and systematic manner, even if by means of an overview, the Church's social teaching, which is the fruit of careful Magisterial reflection and an expression of the Church's constant commitment in fidelity to the grace of salvation wrought in Christ and in loving concern for humanity's destiny. Herein the most relevant theological, philosophical, moral, cultural and pastoral considerations of this teaching are systematically presented as they relate to social questions. In this way, witness is borne to the fruitfulness of the encounter between the Gospel and the problems that mankind encounters on its journey through history. (*Compendium*, 8)

In all, the *Compendium* is some two hundred and fifty pages long (excluding indexes) and is divided into three parts. The first section examines such concepts as God's plan of love for humanity and society, the human person and human rights, and an overview of the principles of social doctrine. The second part focuses on traditional concepts of social doctrine such as work, economics, politics, and peace. The final section consists of recommendations for the implementation of the teachings.

Ten Commandments

With the earlier encyclicals and letters as the *Compendium's* foundation, it is no surprise that such a collection of Church teaching would include a strong environmental component. Indeed, in the second section of the *Compendium* we find the Church's teaching on the relationship between morality and the environment presented in its most comprehensive form to date. In the chapter titled "Safeguarding the Environment," the Pontifical Council for Justice and Peace covers such diverse topics as biblical imperatives, the crisis between humanity and the environment, the use of biotechnology, the importance of potable water, and the need for changes in lifestyles. While the statements at first did not arouse much interest outside of scholarly and theological circles, that changed on November 7, 2005, at a congress on "Ethics and the Environment" at the European University of Rome. At that meeting, Bishop Giampaolo Crepaldi, secretary of the Pontifical Council for Justice and Peace, offered ten principles of environmental ethics drawn from the *Compendium,* which he presented as "ten commandments" (he was clear, however, that these were not to be interpreted as replacing the Ten Commandments God gave to Moses). The media took notice of this new set of "commandments," although the concepts are more guiding principles than a list of dos and don'ts.

The primary message of the Ten Commandments for the Environment presented by Bishop Crepaldi is that humanity must be a responsible steward of God's Creation. Humans are to use the earth, not abuse it, and in doing so become co-creators with God in the process of the formation of a new heaven and new earth. Underlying the Commandments is the sense that all our actions, both on an individual and collective level, should be guided by a balance of conservation and development, with the understanding that the goods of the earth, such as food and water, are to be shared by all, not hoarded by a few. While we will conduct a more detailed examination of each of the Commandments in later chapters, here is an overview:

1. The human being, created in God's image, is placed above all other earthly creatures, which must be used and cared for in a responsible way in cooperation with the divine plan of redemption.

2. Nature must not be reduced to a utilitarian object of manipulation, nor absolutized or placed above human dignity.

3. Ecological responsibility involves the entire planet in a common duty to respect the environment as a collective good, for present and future generations.

4. In dealing with environmental problems, ethics and human dignity should come before technology.

5. Nature is not a sacred or divine reality, removed from human intervention. Thus, human intervention that modifies some characteristics of living things is not wrong, as long as it respects their place in their particular ecosystem.

6. The politics of development must be coordinated with the politics of ecology, and every environmental cost in development projects must be weighed carefully.

7. Ending global poverty is related to the environmental question, remembering that the goods of the earth must be shared equitably.

8. The right to a safe and clean environment needs to be protected through international cooperation and accords.

9. Environmental protection requires a change in lifestyles that reflect moderation and self-control, on a personal and social level. That means moving away from the mindset of consumerism.

10. Environmental issues call for a spiritual response, inspired by the belief that creation is a gift that God has placed into our responsible hands, so that we can use it with loving care. The human person's attitude toward nature should be one of gratitude and gratefulness to the God who has created and supports it.

Pope Benedict and the Ten Commandments for the Environment

Although Benedict XVI did not write the Ten Commandments for the Environment, they reflect the essence of his teaching and message. His off-the-cuff comments and homilies, as well as his speeches, all support them fully. While, as of this writing, he has yet to publish an extensive statement on environmental issues, more documents and references to ecology and global climate crises have been issued under his papacy than anyone would have anticipated. Above all, what makes Benedict unique in the environmental movement is his understanding of the inseparable link between Creation, Redemption, and the environment.

As Bishop Golser said in an interview shortly after his appointment as bishop of the Bolzano-Bressanone diocese:

> Even back when he was the cardinal of Munich, [Pope Benedict] gave homilies in which he lamented that the theology of Creation has been overlooked in the period since the Second

Vatican Council [1962–65]. Post-conciliar theology wanted to emphasize the history of salvation, but for him it was equally important to see that everything, the entire cosmos, has been created in view of Jesus Christ.

In other words, Creation and Redemption go together. From that point of departure, he often goes back to St. Francis of Assisi, even to Marian devotion, with the idea that all of Creation in a way enters into this Marian function of preparing for the arrival of the Redeemer. Everything has been born in order to glorify God.

This is the specific point about our Christian faith, and what sets apart the way the Holy Father approaches this question from the secular environmental movement. Some currents can be pantheistic, or sometimes they downplay the special place of humanity in favor of the concept of this great "Gaia," and so on. People sometimes criticize the Christian vision of the environment for being anthropocentric, but in fact it's theo-centric. We can only understand Creation by seeing it in terms of [the] mystery of the Trinity. Of course, there's also an eschatological dimension, which is that all of Creation must be reborn and presented anew to the Father through Christ.[4]

This is the message Benedict has presented throughout his pontificate. Through both his words and actions, Benedict reminds us:

If we observe what came into being around monasteries, how in those places small paradises, oases of creation were and continue to be born, it becomes evident that these were not only words. Rather, wherever the Creator's Word was properly understood, wherever life was lived with the

redeeming Creator, people strove to save Creation
and not to destroy it.[5]

Finally, it's not surprising that Pope Benedict
would talk about the need to develop "oases of creation" in the world, referring back to monastic influ-
ences. His namesake is, after all, St. Benedict of
Nursia, the founder of Western monasticism, who
himself said: "Listen and attend with the ear of your
heart." Benedict XVI is asking all of us to do just that
in this critical time for our planet and its inhabitants.
Listen and attend . . . before it is too late.

USE,

DON'T

ABUSE

THE BIBLE LAYS OUT THE FUNDAMENTAL MORAL PRINCIPLES OF HOW TO CONFRONT THE ECOLOGICAL QUESTION. **THE HUMAN PERSON, MADE IN GOD'S IMAGE, IS SUPERIOR TO ALL OTHER EARTHLY CREATURES, WHICH SHOULD IN TURN BE USED RESPONSIBLY.** CHRIST'S INCARNATION AND HIS TEACHINGS TESTIFY TO THE VALUE OF NATURE: NOTHING THAT EXISTS IN THIS WORLD IS OUTSIDE THE DIVINE PLAN OF CREATION AND REDEMPTION.

We begin at the beginning: Genesis. The story of Creation. The first of the Ten Commandments for the Environment encourages us to look anew at the first book of the Bible, where the instructions for ethical behavior toward the earth are woven into the very fabric of Creation.

> Then God said: "Let us make man in our image, after our likeness. Let them have dominion over the fish of the sea, the birds of the air, and the cattle, and over all the wild animals and all the creatures that crawl on the ground."
>
> God created man in his image; in the divine image he created him; male and female he created them.
>
> God blessed them, saying: "Be fertile and multiply; fill the earth and subdue it. Have dominion over the fish of the sea, the birds of the air, and all the living things that move on the earth."
>
> God also said: "See, I give you every seed-bearing plant all over the earth and every tree that has seed-bearing fruit on it to be your food; and to all the animals of the land, all the birds of the air, and all the living creatures that crawl on the ground, I give all the green plants for food." And so it happened.
>
> God looked at everything he had made, and he found it very good. (Gen 1:27–31)

> The Lord God then took the man and settled him
> in the garden of Eden, to cultivate and care for it.
> (Gen 2:15)

God put human beings in charge of the earth, to have dominion over the animals and to "cultivate and care" for the land. But almost from the beginning, problems arose. The perfect harmony of humanity and the rest of Creation was ruptured. Early human beings, contrary to Jean-Jacques Rousseau's still lingering theory of the "Noble Savage," did not walk gently on the earth, leaving no mark but a few bent branches and footprints, but used and even exploited it and its other inhabitants. For example, some scientists believe that the woolly mammoths that once roamed the plains of North America were pushed into extinction by overhunting, an idea that runs contrary to the notion that our ancestors lived harmoniously with nature.[1] It is known for sure that the native residents of Wrangel Island, the last bastion of the mammoths, killed the final mammoth on earth about 2000 years ago[2] and that the Maori killed off the entire Moa bird population in New Zealand within probably a few hundred years after their arrival on the island.

Such use and misuse of the land is not limited to small, isolated areas. Among the theories put forth to explain the collapse of the highly developed civilization of the Mayans, which extended over vast parts of what is now Mexico and Central America, is over-exploitation of natural resources, in particular of the rainforest.[3] University of Arizona archaeologist T. Patrick Culbert says pollen recovered from underground debris shows clearly that "there was almost no tropical forest left,"[4] a human-created disaster that certainly contributed to the decline and eventual fall of the culture.

Perhaps the clearest example of premodern environmental destruction lies a little over 2000 miles west of Chile in the middle of the Pacific Ocean. The barren wasteland that is now Easter Island was created entirely by human action. Originally the island was a subtropical paradise, covered with trees and home to innumerable species of animals, but by the time of European contact, deforestation down to the last tree completely destroyed the ecosystem, turning the area into a desolate, rat-infested rock.[5]

These are but a few of the places where premodern humanity has wreaked havoc on the earth, even if it was done out of ignorance and lack of understanding, rather than deliberate malice. The underlying problem, as Pope Benedict has succinctly noted, is that God's original command to "have dominion over the earth" has been sorely corrupted:

> As long as the earth was considered as God's Creation, the task of "subduing" it was never intended as an order to enslave it but rather as a task of being guardians of Creation and developing its gifts; of actively collaborating in God's work ourselves, in the evolution that he ordered in the world so that the gifts of Creation might be appreciated rather than trampled upon and destroyed.[6]

Certainly the gifts of Creation have been these and are being trampled on. Just consider these profoundly unsettling facts:

- Rainforests once covered 14 percent of the earth's land surface; they now cover 6 percent.

- Nearly half of the world's species of plants, animals, and microorganisms will be destroyed or severely threatened over the next quarter-century due to rainforest deforestation.

- Experts estimate that 137 plant, animal, and insect species are lost every single day due to rainforest deforestation. That equates to 50,000 species a year. [7]

- No glaciers will be present in Glacier National Park by 2030.[8]

- 40,000 kilometers of sea ice has already melted in the Arctic.[9]

- Because of the loss of sea ice, polar bears are unable to get to their food sources of ringed seals and are turning to cannibalism to survive.[10]

- By 2032, more than 90 percent of the range of the great apes will suffer from humans' development, including 99 percent of the orangutan range.[11]

- A quarter of the world's mammals and one out of every eight plants face extinction. If current trends continue, half of all species on earth will be gone within one hundred years.[12]

A New Vision

In the face of such frightening prospects, Benedict is telling us—all of us, Christian and non-Christian alike—that we were created to be caregivers, stewards, champions of God's Creation, not despotic rulers. Speaking to the youth of the world in Australia, Benedict reminded them, and all of us, that "God's Creation is one and it is good." He went on to say, "Our world has grown weary of greed, exploitation, and division, of the tedium of false idols and piecemeal responses, and the pain of false promises. Our hearts and minds are yearning for a vision of life where love endures, where gifts are shared, where unity is built, where freedom finds meaning in truth, and where identity is found in respectful communion."[13]

The notion that humanity can, and indeed should, live in "respectful communion" with nature has become increasingly urgent. In the last few decades, a confluence of symptoms combined to alert scientists to the indisputable fact that the earth was sick and getting sicker by the day—rising ocean temperatures, melting glaciers, holes in the ozone layer, vanishing species, unprecedented natural disasters. Perhaps if we had paid attention to Svante Arrhenius, a Swedish scientist who claimed in 1896 that use of fossil fuels could result in global warming, we would not have been so startled in 1988 to learn that the planet was warmer than it had been in a century, a phenomenon dubbed "the Greenhouse Effect."[14]

At about the same time that scientists were sounding environmental alarm bells, Pope John Paul II was pointing out the moral imperative to protect the planet. At his General Audience on January 17, 2001, he said:

> The human creature receives a mission to govern Creation in order to make all its potential shine. Unfortunately, if we scan the regions of our planet, we immediately see that humanity has disappointed God's expectations. Man, especially in our time, has without hesitation devastated wooded plains and valleys, polluted waters, disfigured the earth's habitat, made the air unbreathable, disturbed the hydrogeological and atmospheric systems, turned luxuriant areas into deserts, and undertaken forms of unrestrained industrialization, degrading that "flowerbed"—to use an image from Dante Alighieri (*Paradiso*, XXII, 151)—which is the earth, our dwelling-place. We must therefore encourage and support

the "ecological conversion" which in recent decades has made humanity more sensitive to the catastrophe to which it has been heading. Man is no longer the Creator's "steward", but an autonomous despot, who is finally beginning to understand that he must stop at the edge of the abyss.[15]

Unfortunately, both scientific and papal exhortations were largely ignored when they first began speaking out.

But no longer. Pope Benedict has taken up his predecessor's mantle with an unexpected exigency and clarity. "Our earth is talking to us," he said during a meeting with the clergy of the dioceses of Belluno-Feltre and Treviso in July 2007:

We all see that today man can destroy the foundation of his existence, his Earth. We cannot simply do what we want with this Earth of ours, with what has been entrusted to us. On the contrary, we must respect the inner laws of creation, of this earth, we must learn these laws and obey these laws if we wish to survive. This obedience to the voice of the Earth, of being, is more important for our future happiness than the voices of the moment, the desires of the moment. In short, this is a first criterion to learn: that being itself, our earth, speaks to us and we must listen if we want to survive and decipher the message of the earth.[16]

Creation and Redemption Are Inseparable

What sets Pope Benedict apart from scientists and other world leaders who are expressing deep concern about the future of the earth is that Benedict, as did

John Paul before him, links Creation with Redemption. Above we noted Fr. Golser's question to Benedict in a question-and-answer session in 2007. In his reply to Fr. Golser, Benedict emphasized this link between Creation and Redemption:

> In recent decades, the doctrine of Creation had almost disappeared in theology, it was almost imperceptible. We are now aware of the damage that this has caused. The Redeemer is the Creator, and if we do not proclaim God in his full grandeur—as Creator and as Redeemer—we also diminish the value of the Redemption. Indeed, if God has no role in Creation, if he is relegated merely to a historical context, how can he truly understand the whole of our life? How could he truly bring salvation for humanity in its entirety and for the world in its totality? This is why for me, renewal of the doctrine of Creation, and a new understanding of the inseparability of Creation and Redemption, takes on such great importance. We have to recognize anew: He is the *Creator Spiritus*, the Reason from whom in the beginning everything is born, and of which our own reason is but a spark. It is he, the Creator himself, who entered into history and can still enter into history and act in it, because he is the God of the whole and not just of a part. If we recognize this, obviously what follows is that the Redemption, what it means to be Christian, and simply the Christian faith in itself, always signify responsibility with regard to Creation . . . .
>
> Creation is groaning—we can sense it, we can almost hear it—and it is waiting for human beings who will preserve it in accordance with God. The brutal consumption of Creation begins

where God is missing, where matter has become simply material for us, where we ourselves are the ultimate measure, where everything is simply our property and we consume it only for ourselves. The waste of Creation begins where we no longer recognize any claim beyond ourselves, seeing only ourselves; it begins where there is no longer any dimension of life beyond death, where in this life we have to grab everything and take hold of life with the maximum intensity possible, where we have to possess everything it is possible to possess.

I believe, therefore, that true and effective measures against the waste and destruction of Creation can only be realized and developed, understood and lived, when Creation is considered as beginning with God; when life is considered on the basis of God and has its major dimensions in responsibility before God; life that one day will be given by God in its fullness and never taken away. In giving life, we receive it.[17]

Pope Benedict emphasizes that earthly life and eternal life, Creation and Redemption, are not only linked, but are inseparable. In Christ, we have become "new creatures," as St. Paul says, but through that redemptive process, we are obligated to join creatively with God in "renewing the face of the earth." By becoming man, by walking on the earth, basking in the sun, eating of its produce, and interacting with its wildlife, Jesus affirmed the words of Genesis: "And God saw that it was good."

Even before he was Pope, Benedict wrote about the link between Creation and Redemption:

Two movements are interacting here. One is that of human beings who do not exploit the world and do not want to detach it from the Creator's governance and make it their own property; rather they recognize it as God's gift and built it up in keeping with what it was created for. Conversely, we see that the world, which was created to be at one with its Lord, is not a threat but a gift and a sign of the saving and unifying goodness of God.[18]

Pope John Paul expressed the same thought quite eloquently in his first encyclical:

The Redeemer of the world! In him has been revealed in a new and more wonderful way the fundamental truth concerning Creation to which the Book of Genesis gives witness when it repeats several times: "God saw that it was good." The good has its source in Wisdom and Love. In Jesus Christ the visible world which God created for man—the world that, when sin entered, "was subjected to futility"—recovers again its original link with the divine source of Wisdom and Love. Indeed, "God so loved the world that he gave his only Son." As this link was broken in the man Adam, so in the Man Christ it was re-forged. Are we of the twentieth century not convinced of the overpoweringly eloquent words of the Apostle of the Gentiles concerning the "Creation (that) has been groaning in travail together until now" and "waits with eager longing for the revelation of the sons of God," the Creation that "was subjected to futility"? Does not the previously unknown immense progress—which has taken place especially in the course of this century—in the field of man's dominion over the world itself reveal—to a previously unknown degree—that manifold subjection "to futility"? It is enough to recall certain phenomena, such as the threat of pollution of the natural environment in areas of rapid industrialization, or the armed conflicts continually breaking out over and over again, or the prospects of self-destruction through the use of atomic, hydrogen, neutron, and similar weapons, or the lack of respect for the life of the unborn. The world of the new age, the world of space flights, the world of the previously unattained conquests of science and technology—is it not also the world "groaning in travail" that "waits with eager longing for the revealing of the sons of God"? (*Redemptor Hominis,* 8)

God Found It Very Good

Which returns us to the First Commandment for the Environment. Although humanity stands at the apex of Creation, all of nature is valuable if for no other reason than it reflects the glory and majesty of God. Our responsibility then is to respect Creation, not subjugating it to our whim and will, but tending to it as it fulfills God's own purposes. We are cooperators with the Creator in preserving and maintaining Creation itself.

In a question-and-answer session with journalists aboard the papal plane on his way to World Youth Day 2008 in Australia, Benedict observed,

> In this historical moment, we begin to see that we do need God. We can do so many things, but we cannot create our climate. We thought we could do it, but we cannot do it. We need the gift of the Earth, the gift of water, we need the Creator. The Creator reappears in his Creation. And so we also come to understand that we cannot be really happy, cannot be really promoting

justice for all the world, without a criterion at work in our own ideas, without a God who is just, and gives us the light, and gives us life.[19]

Finally, it is important to recognize the significance of this commandment with regard to our treatment of our fellow members of the animal kingdom. In an interview with journalist Peter Seewald in 2000, Benedict expressed deep concern for the well-being of all animals who share our planet:

> We can see that they are given into our care, that we cannot just do whatever we want with them. Animals, too, are God's creatures, and even if they do not have the same direct relation to God that man has, they are still creatures of his will, creatures we must respect as companions in creation and as important elements in the creation. . . . Certainly, a sort of industrial use of creatures, so that geese are fed in such a way as to produce as large a liver as possible, or hens live so packed together that they become just caricatures of birds, this degrading of living creatures to a commodity seems to me in fact to contradict the relationship of mutuality that comes across in the Bible.[20]

And so we end where we began—with Genesis. As Benedict said in his introductory remarks to the young in Australia:

> The views afforded of our planet from the air [on the flight to Australia] were truly wondrous. The sparkle of the Mediterranean, the grandeur of the north African desert, the lushness of Asia's forestation, the vastness of the Pacific Ocean, the horizon upon which the sun rose and set, and the majestic splendor of Australia's natural beauty which I have been able to enjoy these last couple of days; these all evoke a profound sense of awe.

It is as though one catches glimpses of the Genesis Creation story—light and darkness, the sun and the moon, the waters, the earth, and living creatures; all of which are "good" in God's eyes (cf. Gen 1:1—2:4). Immersed in such beauty, who could not echo the words of the Psalmist in praise of the Creator: "how majestic is your name in all the earth?" (Ps 8:1).[21]

Indeed, it is a wonder-filled and wonderful world that has been entrusted to our care. Now it is up to us to make sure that it lasts as long as we do.

LITTLE LESS

THAN

A GOD

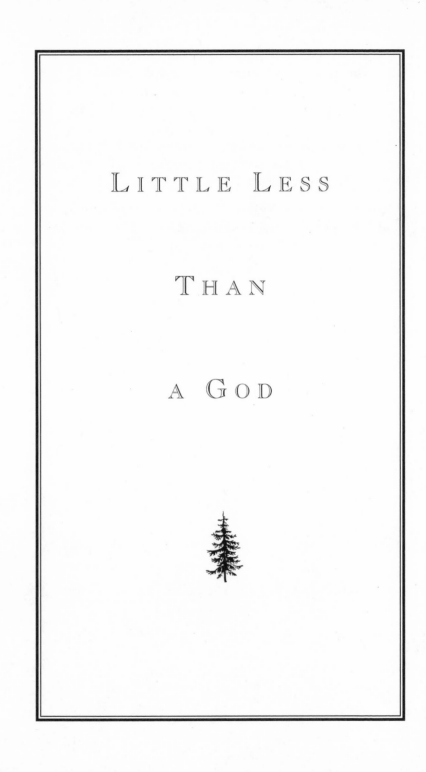

THE SOCIAL TEACHING OF THE CHURCH RECALLS TWO FUNDAMENTAL POINTS. **WE SHOULD NOT REDUCE NATURE TO A MERE INSTRUMENT TO BE MANIPULATED AND EXPLOITED. NOR SHOULD WE MAKE NATURE AN ABSOLUTE VALUE,** OR PUT IT ABOVE THE DIGNITY OF THE HUMAN PERSON.

Since the publication of Charles Darwin's *The Origin of Species* in 1859 and its follow-up *The Descent of Man* twelve years later, Darwin's theory of "the descent of man from some lower form" has seemingly placed science and religion at odds. Right in the center of the controversy is what might be called the question of the "dignity of the human person." As Psalm 8 says, "What are humans that you are mindful of them, mere mortals that you care for them? Yet you have made them little less than a god, crowned them with glory and honor." Moreover, the next verses seem to give humanity its marching orders: "You have given them rule over the works of your hands, put all things at their feet: All sheep and oxen, even the beasts of the field, the birds of the air, the fish of the sea, and whatever swims the paths of the seas."

Some have interpreted biblical passages such as this to mean not only that humans are superior to the rest of Creation, but that humans and the rest of Creation have little in common, and certainly do not share a common origin. Beginning with Darwin, however, science began to assemble an almost unassailable body of evidence indicating that humans did, indeed, share a common ancestry with the rest of life on the planet. The mechanics of gene mutation, natural selection, and species change over time were being supported by various new and old disciplines including archaeology, biology, and genetics. It was becoming evident to most scientists that some form of evolution had been and was still taking place. One of the more startling discoveries seemed to indicate that the genus *Homo*, of which modern man, *Homo sapiens sapiens*, is a part, had other lines which are now extinct. These include *Homo habilis*, which lived from about 2.4 to 1.4 million years ago in Africa, *Homo erectus*, which inhabited Asia, and *Homo neanderthalensis*, which lived in what is now the Middle East and Europe from 250,000 to as recent as 30,000 years ago, overlapping modern humans by as much as 40,000 years.[1] On the basis of findings such as these, some scientists today argue that humans lack any unique dignity vis-à-vis the rest of Creation. Certain biblical literalists, on the other hand, argue that the scientific discoveries must be in error, since they evidently disagree with scripture.

In this controversy brewing between a certain literalist reading of scripture and scientific research lies the core problem addressed by the Second Commandment for the Environment. If human beings have nothing in common with the rest of life on the planet, then nature is merely a tool to be used as humans so desire. The world and its resources can be altered, changed, exploited, and consumed at will since humanity is not only substantially superior to the earth, but completely unrelated to it. On the other hand, if human beings are merely another life form on the planet, lacking any special dignity, then nature itself can be viewed as the supreme force and humanity should make no attempt to impose its will on the natural order. (See Chapter 7 for a discussion of nature as divine.)

Both points of view are flawed, according to the teaching of the Church. The human person is, indeed, the apex of Creation but is, at the same time, an integral part of that same Creation. Therefore, humanity does not have the right to wantonly impose its whims and will on nature, but neither is humankind required to submit passively to its fluctuations.

Creation and Evolution

Father Rafael Pascual, director of the master's program in Science and Faith at the Regina Apostolorum Pontifical University in Rome, explained the Magisterium's view of evolution in a 2005 interview with Zenit.org. Fr. Pascual explained:

> For the Church, in principle, there is no incompatibility between the truth of Creation and the scientific theory of evolution. God could have created a world in evolution, which in itself does not take anything away from divine causality; on the contrary, it can focus on it better as regards its wealth and potentiality. . . . On the question of the origin of the human being, an evolutionary process could be admitted in regard to his corporeal nature, but in the case of the soul, because it is spiritual, a direct creative action is required on the part of God, given that what is spiritual cannot be initiated by something that is not spiritual. . . . The fact of being created and loved immediately by God is the only thing that can justify, in the last instance, the dignity of the human being. . . . The human being is the only creature that God wanted for its own sake; he [the human] is an end in himself, and cannot be treated as a means to reach any other end, no matter how noble it is or seems to be.[2]

Pope Benedict surprised some when the media reported early in his papacy that he supported evolution, but his understanding of the complex role between human beings and nature, Creation and evolution, is more nuanced than a simple acceptance of evolutionary theory per se. In a speech to the Pontifical Academy of Sciences on October 31, 2008, he stated:

> Questions concerning the relationship between science's reading of the world and the reading offered by Christian Revelation naturally arise. My predecessors Pope Pius XII and Pope John Paul II noted that there is no opposition between faith's understanding of Creation and the evidence of the empirical science. . . . In order to develop and evolve, the world must first be, and thus have come from nothing into being. It must be created, in other words, by the first Being who is such by essence.[3]

It's clear that, for Benedict, Creation and evolution can be understood as complementary, in the sense that evolution helps to "complete" the work of Creation. As far back as 1981, when he was the archbishop of Munich, Cardinal Joseph Ratzinger wrote:

> The exact formula is Creation and evolution, because both respond to two different questions. The account of the dust of the earth and the breath of God, does not in fact tell us how man originated. It tells us that it is man. It speaks to us of his most profound origin, illustrates the plan that is behind him. Vice versa, the theory of evolution tries to define and describe biological processes. However, it does not succeed in explaining the origin of the "project" man, to explain his interior provenance and his essence.

We are faced therefore with two questions that complement, not exclude each other.[4]

In addressing his speech to the Pontifical Academy of Sciences, Pope Benedict further elucidated his thoughts on evolution and nature:

> To "evolve" literally means "to unroll a scroll," that is, to read a book. The imagery of nature as a book has its roots in Christianity and has been held dear by many scientists. Galileo saw nature as a book whose author is God in the same way that Scripture has God as its author. It is a book whose history, whose evolution, whose "writing" and meaning, we "read" according to the different approaches of the sciences, while all the time presupposing the foundational presence of the author who has wished to reveal himself therein. This image also helps us to understand that the world, far from originating out of chaos, resembles an ordered book; it is a cosmos.[5]

Evolution and Faith

What is quite clear is that for Pope Benedict, any acceptable theory of evolution will have to admit its limitations and leave room for philosophy and faith when it comes to ultimate questions about the meaning and origin of life. In 1999 then-Cardinal Ratzinger reflected at length on the relationships between evolutionary science, philosophy, and faith in a lecture at the Sorbonne in Paris, subsequently published in Cardinal Ratzinger's book *Truth and Tolerance*:

> The theory of evolution has increasingly emerged as the way . . . to make "the hypothesis of God" (Laplace) superfluous, and to formulate a

strictly "scientific" explanation of the world. . . .
The question that has now to be put certainly
delves deeper: it is whether the theory of evolution can be presented as a universal theory concerning all reality, beyond which further
questions about the origin and the nature of
things are no longer admissible and indeed no
longer necessary, or whether such ultimate questions do not after all go beyond the realm of what
can be entirely the object of research and knowl-
edge by natural science.[6]

As Benedict explains, Christianity, along with
many philosophers, both Christian and non-
Christian, affirms a rational order to Creation that
ultimately comes from the Creator.

The question is whether reason, or rationality,
stands at the beginning of all things and is
grounded in the basis of all things or not. The
question is whether reality originated on the
basis of chance and necessity . . . and, thus, from
what is irrational . . . or whether the principle
that represents the fundamental conviction of
Christian faith and of its philosophy remains
true: *"In principio erat Verbum"*—at the beginning
of all things stands the creative power of reason.
Now as then, Christian faith represents the
choice in favor of the priority of reason and of
rationality.[7]

Benedict further argues that this choice between,
on one hand, Creation as the work of a Creator, the
Word, the Logos, and, on the other hand, Creation as
an irrational product of chance has significance not
just on a speculative plane, but also for our ethical
outlook and conduct.

Every explanation of reality that cannot at the same time provide a meaningful and comprehensible basis for ethics necessarily remains inadequate. Now the theory of evolution . . . has in fact been used for an attempt at a new ethos based on evolution. Yet this evolutionary ethic that inevitably takes as its key concept the model of selectivity, that is, the struggle for survival, the victory of the fittest, successful adaptation, has little comfort to offer. Even when people try to make it more attractive in various ways, it ultimately remains a bloodthirsty ethic. Here, the attempt to distill rationality out of what is in itself irrational quite visibly fails. All this is of very little use for an ethic of universal peace, of practical love of one's neighbor, and of the necessary overcoming of oneself, which is what we need.[8]

Evolution, then, on its own cannot tell us where we come from, nor can it guide our behavior toward our neighbor. In order for us to properly understand such things, theories of evolution, like all scientific thought, must always be brought into harmony with faith. When such a harmony is achieved, the result can be beautiful. As Benedict explained in 2005:

Through the reason of Creation, God himself looks at us. Physics, biology, the natural sciences in general, have given us a new, unheard-of account of Creation, with grandiose and new images, which enable us to recognize the face of the Creator and make us know again: Yes, in the beginning and deep down in every being is the Creator Spirit. The world is not the product of darkness and the absurd. It comes from an intelligence, from a freedom, from a beauty that is love. To acknowledge this, infuses in us the courage that enables us to live, that makes us capable of confidently facing life's venture."[9]

It is no wonder then that in his homily at the start of his Petrine ministry, he said: "We are not some casual and meaningless product of evolution. Each of us is the result of a thought of God. Each of us is willed, each of us is loved, each of us is necessary."[10]

It is precisely because of that love that we can neither allow nature to be elevated above humanity, nor can we allow nature to be reduced to a mere instrument to be manipulated and exploited. We are "made in the image and likeness of God" who is both the Creator and, through the incarnation of Jesus, a part of his own Creation as well. Because of our unique position as "little less than a god," we, too, serve both as co-creators and stewards of this world. Pope Benedict reminds us that we must do both responsibly if we are to live well on this planet.

ONE FOR ALL,

ALL FOR

ONE

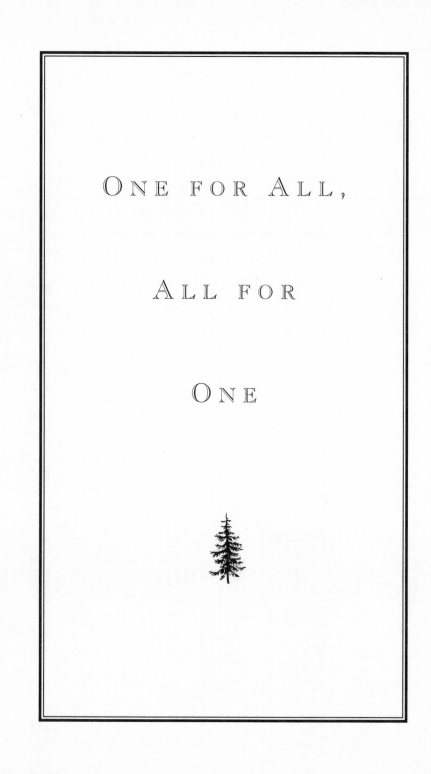

**THE QUESTION OF THE ENVIRONMENT
ENTAILS THE WHOLE PLANET,** AS IT IS A
COLLECTIVE GOOD. OUR RESPONSIBILITY
TOWARD ECOLOGY EXTENDS TO FUTURE
GENERATIONS.

hen Pope Benedict speaks of the importance of caring for the environment, he is not addressing only certain elite nations or even people of a particular religious persuasion. He makes it clear that he is talking to the inhabitants of the entire planet. As he said in his message for World Peace Day 2009: "Does not every one of us sense deep within his or her conscience a call to make a personal contribution to the common good and to peace in society?"[1] Indeed, it is fitting that he calls on every one of us, for our differences are literally only skin deep. No substantial differences can be found at the DNA level among any modern humans.[2] We are all, quite literally, made in the same image of the same God.

Moreover, scientists are realizing that we and our planet are interconnected in ways that were unheard of even a hundred years ago. The "butterfly effect," a component of Chaos Theory that suggests a butterfly flapping its wings can affect the weather on the other side of the globe, has entered the popular lexicon and is sometimes joked about, but it captures a fundamental truth. Perhaps the movement of a single butterfly's wings doesn't actually do much to change the path of a hurricane, but the fact remains we really are all in this together. What we do to one part of the world has a profound and lasting effect on the rest of the globe.

As the *Compendium* puts it:

Care for the environment represents a challenge for all of humanity. It is a matter of a common and universal duty, that of respecting a common good, destined for all, by preventing anyone from using with impunity the different categories of beings, whether living or inanimate—animals, plants, the natural elements—simply as one wishes, according to one's own economic needs. It is a responsibility that must mature on the basis of the global dimension of the present ecological crisis and the consequent necessity to meet it on a worldwide level, since all beings are interdependent in the universal order established by the Creator. One must take into account the nature of each being and of its mutual connection in an ordered system, which is precisely the "cosmos." (*Compendium*, 466)

We Are Interconnected

The global dimension of ecological crises can be readily seen in the nuclear reactor accident at Chernobyl in 1986. As explained in TORCH (The Other Report on Chernobyl):

Early on April 26 1986, two explosions in Chernobyl unit 4 completely destroyed the reactor. The explosions sent large clouds of radioactive gases and debris 7–9 kilometres into the atmosphere. About 30% of the reactor's 190 tons of fuel was distributed over the reactor building and surrounding areas and about 1–2% was ejected into the atmosphere. The reactor's inventory of radioactive gases was released at this time. The subsequent fire, fuelled by 1,700 tons of graphite moderator, lasted for eight days.[3]

At first it didn't seem all that horrendous, except for the people living in the immediate area. But soon the world realized that the long-term effects were catastrophic. The nuclear meltdown produced a radioactive cloud that affected not only Russia and Eastern Europe, but Western Europe as well. The TORCH report continues:

> In terms of their surface areas, Belarus (22% of its land area) and Austria (13%) were most affected by higher levels of contamination. Other countries were seriously affected; for example, more than 5% of Ukraine, Finland and Sweden were contaminated to high levels. More than 80% of Moldova, the European part of Turkey, Slovenia, Switzerland, Austria and the Slovak Republic were contaminated to lower levels. And 44% of Germany and 34% of the UK were similarly affected.[4]

All in all, nearly 40 percent of the surface area of Europe and more than one million people were exposed to radiation from this one accident. As late as 2006, the effects were still showing up in food sources in natural or near-natural environments from Sweden and Finland to Germany, Austria, Italy, Lithuania, and Poland.[5]

More than anything else in modern times, Chernobyl shows that the actions of humanity have a profound, lasting, and potentially devastating effect on every living creature on earth.

The Common Good

That's the discouraging news. The encouraging news is that just as oil spills, rainforest destruction, and CO_2 emissions impact the entire world and its population, so our positive actions can contribute to the collective good.

Pope Benedict seems to understand the need for positive encouragement to work for this collective good. In 2007, at a speech in the courtyard of the papal summer residence at Castel Gondolfo, he urged that "cooperation on everyone's part be intensified in order to promote the common good and the development and safeguard[ing] of creation." At that time, the Holy Father said, "In the last two decades, thanks to exemplary collaboration between politicians, scientists, and economists within the international community, important results have been obtained with positive repercussions on present and future generations."[6]

In his address to the U.N. on sustainable development, Archbishop Celestino Migliore, Apostolic Nuncio and Permanent Observer of the Holy See to the United Nations, also emphasized the importance of global cooperation with regard to protecting the environment. He stated:

> The responsibility to protect the climate should be based on the alliance between the principles of subsidiarity and global solidarity. In a world so interconnected as today, we are witnessing the rapid expansion of a series of challenges in many areas of human life, from food crises to financial turmoil. Such crises have revealed the limited national resources and capacities to deal with them adequately, and the increasing need for collective action by the international community. The current negotiations on the UN Framework Convention on Climate Change are a good example of how responsibility to protect, subsidiarity, and global solidarity are strongly

intertwined with each other, a fact that we ought to take into account as we consider the protection of the global climate for present and future generations.[7]

For Future Generations

For Benedict, the idea that care for the environment must be handled globally is closely connected to the understanding that ecological responsibility extends to the next generations, both in the sense that we must preserve the earth for those who will follow us and that we must raise the awareness among the youth of the world so that they, too, understand the important work to be done in this critical area.

This emphasis is a bit surprising to some. When Cardinal Joseph Ratzinger was elected the pontiff, the days of easy papal rapport with youth were assumed to be over. Pope John Paul II loved to be with young people. Even in his last years, he was clearly energized by being in their presence, and they seemed to love being with him equally as much. Pictures abound of his holding and playing with children and youth of all ages. But he had a particular affection for teens and college-aged students. By beginning the tradition of World Youth Day in 1986, he ensured that young people would be officially recognized as an integral and essential part of the Church.

In his inaugural speech introducing the first World Youth Day, John Paul called them "the hope of the Church," adding, "Yes, precisely you, because on you depends the future, on you depends also the end of this millennium and the beginning of the next. So do not be passive; take up your responsibilities in all the fields open to you in our world!"[8]

The easy rapport between the pontiff and young people was expected to diminish when Benedict was elected. He was seen as an aloof, somewhat stern academic theologian who preferred classical music and weighty tomes to interaction with people. He wasn't expected to have much to do with the youth of the world, the assumption being that he would prefer the company of fellow intellectuals and clerics.

What people were forgetting, however, is that before Cardinal Ratzinger became the head of the doctrinal institution for the defense of the faith, he was a teacher, a professor of philosophy and theology. The exuberance and optimism of students is part of his lifeblood. While he might not be one to swoop up babies and chuckle over toddlers, he obviously appreciates the exchanges of ideas and fresh enthusiasm offered by the young. So it wasn't really all that surprising that he has met with young people almost since the beginning of his papacy, nor that one of his first major trips took him to World Youth Day in Australia in 2008.

Nor indeed was it unexpected that the environment was high on his list of concerns to bring to the attention of the hundreds of thousands who gathered in Sydney that summer. For Benedict, World Youth Day was an ideal setting to further promulgate his "green" goals. Even on the papal plane on the way to New South Wales, he mentioned environmental issues three times in a brief fifteen minute press conference with reporters.[9] He first spoke about our need for the "gift of the Earth, the gift of water." In response to a question about climate change, he said, "Certainly this problem will be very present at this World Youth Day, because we're talking about the

Holy Spirit, and in consequence, about Creation and our responsibilities with regard to Creation." And finally he concluded, "It's not my intention to enter into the technical questions, which politicians and specialists have to resolve, but to offer essential impulses for seeing the responsibility, for being capable of responding to this great challenge: rediscovering in Creation the face of the Creator, rediscovering our responsibility before the Creator for the Creation which he has entrusted to us, forming the ethical capacity for a style of life that's necessary to assume if we want to address the problem posed by this situation and if we really want to arrive at positive solutions."[10]

Upon his arrival in Australia, the Pope began by observing the remarkable audience that greeted him: "Standing before me I see a vibrant image of the universal Church. The variety of nations and cultures from which you hail shows that indeed Christ's Good News is for everyone; it has reached the ends of the earth."[11] He went on to say that the "Psalmist prays: 'when you send forth your Spirit, they are created, and you renew the face of the earth' (Ps 104:30). It is my firm belief that young people are called to be instruments of that renewal."[12]

Once on the ground, starting with his opening remarks, Benedict integrated his environmental concerns with his pastoral reflections, reiterating his belief that not only will the youth inherit the earth, but they also must be ready and willing to take over responsibility for its care and governance.

> Many young people today lack hope. They are perplexed by the questions that present themselves ever more urgently in a confusing world, and they

are often uncertain which way to turn for answers. They see poverty and injustice and they long to find solutions. They are challenged by the arguments of those who deny the existence of God and they wonder how to respond. They see great damage done to the natural environment through human greed and they struggle to find ways to live in greater harmony with nature and with one another.[13]

Benedict elaborated on this environmental message in another speech during his time in Australia:

Perhaps reluctantly we come to acknowledge that there are . . . scars which mark the surface of our earth: erosion, deforestation, the squandering of the world's mineral and ocean resources in order to fuel an insatiable consumption. Some of you come from island nations whose very existence is threatened by rising water levels; others from nations suffering the effects of devastating drought. God's wondrous Creation is sometimes experienced as almost hostile to its stewards, even something dangerous. How can what is "good" appear so threatening?[14]

All of this is in keeping with the overall emphasis that sets Benedict apart from others who recognize and warn against environmental destruction—the link of Creation to the Creator: "My dear friends, God's Creation is one and it is good. The concerns for non-violence, sustainable development, justice and peace, and care for our environment are of vital importance for humanity."[15]

Reason for Hope

It is this conviction in the goodness of God's Creation that grounds the strong sense of hope that pervades Benedict's environmental outlook. Where some look at the bleakness of the moment and despair, Benedict possesses a faith and hope in divine purpose and providence. As he said to the youth in Australia:

> Dear friends, life is not governed by chance; it is not random. Your very existence has been willed by God, blessed and given a purpose (cf. Gen 1:28)! Life is not just a succession of events or experiences, helpful though many of them are. It is a search for the true, the good, and the beautiful. It is to this end that we make our choices; it is for this that we exercise our freedom; it is in this—in truth, in goodness, and in beauty—that we find happiness and joy. Do not be fooled by those who see you as just another consumer in a market of undifferentiated possibilities, where choice itself becomes the good, novelty usurps beauty, and subjective experience displaces truth.[16]

Pope Benedict continually reminds future generations that we, young and old alike, must share a common vision and work toward a common goal:

> I know that many of you are generously dedicated to witnessing to your faith in the various social environments, active as volunteers and working to promote the common good, peace and justice in every community. There is no doubt that one of the fields in which it seems urgent to take action is that of safeguarding Creation. The future of the planet is entrusted to the new generations,

in which there are evident signs of a development that has not always been able to protect the delicate balances of nature. Before it is too late, it is necessary to make courageous decisions that can recreate a strong alliance between humankind and the earth. A decisive yes is needed to protect Creation and also a strong commitment to reverse those trends which risk leading to irreversibly degrading situations.[17]

Ultimately, however, Benedict sees an even grander picture—the indissoluble link between care for the earth and world peace.

Alongside the ecology of nature, there exists what can be called a "human" ecology, which in turn demands a "social" ecology. All this means that humanity, if it truly desires peace, must be increasingly conscious of the links between natural ecology, or respect for nature, and human ecology. Experience shows that *disregard for the environment always harms human coexistence,* and vice versa. It becomes more and more evident that there is an inseparable link between peace with Creation and peace among men. Both of these presuppose peace with God.[18]

One gets the sense that one of Benedict's goals is to unite a broken and bellicose world, troubled by religious bigotry and ripped by war, through a mutual understanding that if we do not work together to save the planet, there will be no planet to save.

Our hearts and minds are yearning for a vision of life where love endures, where gifts are shared, where unity is built, where freedom finds meaning in truth, and where identity is found in respectful communion. This is the work of the Holy Spirit! This is the hope held out by the

Gospel of Jesus Christ. It is to bear witness to this reality that you were created anew at Baptism and strengthened through the gifts of the Spirit at Confirmation![19]

Or as he said when he was still the Prefect of the Congregation for the Doctrine of the Faith: "We can win the future only if we do not lose Creation."[20]

IT'S NOT

A BRAVE

NEW WORLD

IT IS NECESSARY TO CONFIRM BOTH THE PRIMACY OF ETHICS AND THE RIGHTS OF MAN OVER TECHNOLOGY, THUS PRESERVING HUMAN DIGNITY. **THE CENTRAL POINT OF REFERENCE FOR ALL SCIENTIFIC AND TECHNICAL APPLICATIONS MUST BE RESPECT FOR THE HUMAN PERSON,** WHO IN TURN SHOULD TREAT THE OTHER CREATED BEINGS WITH RESPECT.

Aldous Huxley's bleak novel *Brave New World* has served as a cautionary tale against the over-investment of society in technology since its publication in 1932. The world of AD 2540 he envisioned is eerily prescient of our current times, in particular the control of reproduction and the relentless emphasis on consumerism, hedonism, and science.

It is precisely this future/present that this fourth Commandment for the Environment addresses. This Commandment rests on the bedrock of respect for life, both human and non-human, and the importance of protecting the earth for future generations, themes that lie close to the heart of Pope Benedict.

Pope Benedict has surprised some who assumed that, because of his conservative approach to faith and doctrine during his tenure as Prefect of the Congregation for the Doctrine of the Faith, he would be a technophobe opposed to modernization and progress. Nothing could be further from the truth. The implementation of solar panels at the Vatican, his praise of advances in medicine[1] and the Vatican's use of modern methods of communication including e-mail and SMS for breaking news are but a few indications that he is supportive of improvements that positively impact our world.

Notwithstanding his progressive stance on many aspects of modernization, Benedict is well aware of the dangers of science and technology. As he told the

Italian Christian Workers' Association, "We live in a time in which science and technology offer extraordinary possibilities for improving everyone's existence. But a distorted use of this power can seriously and irreparably threaten the destiny of life itself."[2]

To understand Benedict's point of view regarding technology and science, it is helpful to refer back to the teachings in the *Compendium*:

> The Magisterium has repeatedly emphasized that the Catholic Church is in no way opposed to progress, rather she considers "science and technology are a wonderful product of a God-given human creativity, since they have provided us with wonderful possibilities, and we all gratefully benefit from them." For this reason, "as people who believe in God, who saw that nature which he had created was 'good', we rejoice in the technological and economic progress which people, using their intelligence, have managed to make."
> (*Compendium*, 475)

Indeed, much good has come from technological advancements, starting with such basic but essential innovations as harnessing fire and inventing the wheel all the way up to the printing press and the Internet. Many inventions have made life much easier and safer for all of us, including advances in modern medicine, transportation, and communication. But, as Pope Benedict warns, all progress is not always for the best. As he wrote in *Values in a Time of Upheaval*,

> Progress has always been a word with a mythical ring. It continues to be portrayed insistently as the norm of political activity and of human behavior in general and as their highest moral qualifications. Anyone who looks even at only

the last hundred years cannot deny that immense progress has been made in medicine, in technology, and in the understanding and harnessing of the forces of nature, and one may hope for further progress. At the same time, however, the ambivalence of this progress is obvious. Progress is beginning to put Creation—the basis of our existence—at risk; it creates inequality among human beings and it generates ever new threats to the world and humanity. This makes moral controls of progress indispensable.[3]

Creation at Risk

Some of the ways that progress, especially in the scientific realm, is putting Creation at risk appear to come directly from a science-fiction movie. For instance, the thousands of chemical compounds, including female hormones from birth control pills, that are being released into the environment are having devastating effects. A CHEM (Chemicals, Health, and Environment Monitoring) Trust report from Britain (CHEM Trust is a nonprofit, UK-based organization devoted to "protecting humans and wildlife from harmful chemicals") indicates that in British lowland rivers, 50 percent of male fish were found to be growing eggs in their testes. Other discovered anomalies include hermaphrodite polar bears and deer with abnormal antler growth.[4]

Another arena in which technology may be opening a new Pandora's box is the creation of GMOs (Genetically Modified Organisms). By combining genes from different organisms through recombinant DNA technology, a new organism that is "genetically modified," "genetically engineered," or "transgenic" is created. For instance, genes from daffodils and a bacterium have been introduced into rice to increase amounts of Vitamin A.[5] Such GMOs range from the bizarre, such a glow-in-the-dark cat,[6] to the practical, such as pesticide- and pest-resistant crops.

More than likely, the editors of the *Compendium* had technologies such as GMOs in mind when they wrote the following:

> The Magisterium's considerations regarding science and technology in general can also be applied to the environment and agriculture. The Church appreciates the advantages that result—and can still result—from the study and applications of molecular biology, supplemented by other disciplines such as genetics and its technological application in agriculture and industry. In fact, technology could be a priceless tool in solving many serious problems, in the first place those of hunger and disease, through the production of more advanced and vigorous strains of plants, and through the production of valuable medicines. It is important, however, to repeat the concept of "proper application," for we know that this potential is not neutral: it can be used either for man's progress or for his degradation. For this reason, it is necessary to maintain an attitude of prudence and attentively sift out the nature, end, and means of the various forms of applied technology. Scientists, therefore, must truly use their research and technical skill in the service of humanity, being able to subordinate them to moral principles and values, which respect and realize in its fullness the dignity of man. (*Compendium*, 458)

While it is beyond the scope of this book to examine in-depth the scientific evidence concerning the dangers of GMOs and the issues of morality surrounding them, it is important to note that genetically modified plants *are* entering the food chain in ever increasing numbers. Tomatoes, soybeans, corn, potatoes, sugar beets, sugar cane, and rice are among those in current production. In 2006, 252 million acres of transgenic crops were planted in twenty-two countries by 10.3 million farmers. New plants—and animals—on the horizon include a sweet potato resistant to a virus that could decimate most of the African harvest, rice with increased iron, bananas that produce human vaccines against infectious diseases such as hepatitis B, fish that mature more quickly, cows that are resistant to bovine spongiform encephalopathy (mad cow disease), and fruit and nut trees that yield years earlier than unmodified trees.[7]

While consumption of genetically modified foods has not yet been shown to have health risks to humans, other side effects are being noted. For instance, some studies indicate that pollen from genetically modified corn can cause high mortality rates in monarch butterfly caterpillars. Although monarch caterpillars eat milkweed plants, not corn, the corn pollen is easily blown onto other plants where it can be eaten by the caterpillars.[8] There is already ample evidence that GMOs will have a negative effect on animal and human life. In essence, the entire planet and its inhabitants are being used as test subjects for this new technology.

The *Compendium* warns particularly against just such actions:

> A central point of reference for every scientific and technological application is respect for men and women, which must also be accompanied by

a necessary attitude of respect for other living creatures. Even when thought is given to making some change in them, one must take into account the nature of each being and of its mutual connection in an ordered system. In this sense, the formidable possibilities of biological research raise grave concerns, in that we are not yet in a position to assess the biological disturbance that could result from indiscriminate genetic manipulation and from the unscrupulous development of new forms of plant and animal life, to say nothing of unacceptable experimentation regarding the origins of human life itself. In fact, it is now clear that the application of these discoveries in the fields of industry and agriculture have produced harmful long-term effects. This has led to the painful realization that we cannot interfere in one area of the ecosystem without paying due attention both to the consequences of such interference in other areas and to the well-being of future generations. (*Compendium*, 459)

Unrestrained Experimentation

Perhaps the most frightening aspect of the new gene manipulation involves chimeras, the physical mixing of cells from two different organisms. Named after a mythological monster described in the *Iliad* as being a lion in front, a snake behind, and a goat in the middle, chimeras are not the same as hybrids. Hybrids are the result of mating between two species, such as a jackass and mare, which produces an offspring, in this case, a mule. Each cell in a mule's body contains both horse and donkey chromosomes. Chimeras, on the other hand, are the result of physically recombining cells to create a new organism. Each individual cell retains its own chromosomal pattern. One way to think of it is that a chimera is like a jigsaw puzzle made from two different pictures cut from the same pattern. A single puzzle can result, but the picture will have distinct elements from both pictures. A hybrid is more like a puzzle completed from two boxes which have only slightly different versions of the same picture. The finished product will be one complete picture, but may show color, shading, or other variations.

A sheep/goat (geep) and rat/mouse chimera have been made, and some Chinese scientists claim to have created a human/rabbit chimera that was destroyed while still at the multiple cell stage. In 2007, a researcher at the University of Nevada's School of Medicine said he had successfully created the world's first "human-sheep chimera," which has 15 percent human cells and 85 percent animal cells[9], and other scientists are working on a mouse/human chimera whose brain cells would be entirely human. Proponents of the process claim that it may provide a source of organs for transplanting, but the moral implications of creating human/animal combinations are more than troubling, as leaders of the Church are well aware.

Cardinal Justin Rigali, chairman of the bishops' Committee on Pro-Life Activities, expressed the Vatican's view on the prohibition of animal/human creations by saying, "While this subject may seem like science fiction to many, the threat is all too real. . . . The alleged promise of embryonic stem cells has already been used in attempts to justify destroying human embryos, and even to justify creating them solely for destructive research. Now, the same utilitarian argument is being used to justify an especially

troubling form of genetic manipulation, to create part-
ly human creatures as mere objects for research or
commercial use. Nothing more radically undermines
human dignity than a project that can make it impos-
sible to determine what is human and what is not."[10]

Benedict himself seems to have such unrestrained
experimentation in mind when he writes:

> Previously human beings could only transform
> particular things in nature; nature as such was
> not the object but rather the presupposition of
> their activity. Now, however, it itself has been
> delivered over to them *in toto*. Yet, as a result,
> they suddenly see themselves as imperiled as
> never before. The reason for this lies in the atti-
> tude that views Creation only as the product of
> chance and necessity. Thus it has no law, no
> direction of its own. The inner rhythm that we
> infer from the scriptural account—the rhythm of
> worship, which is the rhythm of history of God's
> love for humankind—is stilled. Today we can see
> without any difficulty the horrible consequences
> of this attitude.[11]

What Pope Benedict continually asserts is that
humanity, while having the right and even the duty
to co-create with God, must never, in the words of the
Compendium, "make arbitrary use of the earth, sub-
jecting it without restraint to his will, as though it did
not have its own requisites and a prior God-given purpose, which man can indeed develop but must not
betray" (*Compendium*, 460). When the human person
acts in this way, "instead of carrying out his role as a
co-operator with God in the work of Creation, [he] sets
himself up in place of God and thus ends up provok-
ing a rebellion on the part of nature, which is more

tyrannized than governed by him" (*Compendium*, 460).

Warning the world of the dangers of placing technological progress over human rights is a responsibility Pope Benedict takes seriously, not just as the leader of the world's Catholics, but as a spokesperson for morality worldwide. As he and Patriarch Bartholomew I said in their common statement:

> In the face of the great threats to the natural environment, we want to express our concern at the negative consequences for humanity and for the whole of Creation which can result from economic and technological progress that does not know its limits. As religious leaders, we consider it one of our duties to encourage and to support all efforts made to protect God's Creation, and to bequeath to future generations a world in which they will be able to live.[12]

Perhaps Huxley had it right after all when he had his character The Director say, "These are unpleasant facts; I know it. But then most historical facts are unpleasant." Pope Benedict wants to be sure we face these unpleasant historical facts before it becomes too late for all of us.

GAIA

ISN'T

GOD

NATURE MUST NOT BE REGARDED AS A REALITY THAT IS DIVINE IN ITSELF, REMOVED FROM HUMAN ACTION. IT IS, RATHER, A GIFT OFFERED BY OUR CREATOR TO THE HUMAN COMMUNITY, GIVEN TO HUMAN INTELLIGENCE AND MORAL RESPONSIBILITY. IT FOLLOWS, THEN, THAT IT IS NOT ILLICIT TO MODIFY THE ECOSYSTEM, SO LONG AS THIS IS DONE WITHIN THE CONTEXT OF A RESPECT FOR ITS ORDER AND BEAUTY, AND TAKING INTO CONSIDERATION THE UTILITY OF EVERY CREATURE.

In Greek mythology, Gaia, Mother Earth, was a primordial chthonic being, born out of Chaos, the great void of emptiness. From her virginal womb, Pontus, the sea, and Uranus, the sky, were born. Then, with Uranus as her husband, she bore the twelve Titans, godlike giants who personify the forces of nature.

In modern times, Gaia has been resurrected through the Gaia hypothesis. First formulated in the 1960s and refined in the 1970s by James Lovelock, the Gaia hypothesis suggests that the very earth we live on is a living being. Just as the cells of our body make up one organism, so too the very rocks, seas, plants, and animals make up one gigantic living creature more ancient and more complicated than we previously imagined. Hence the reference back to the original Earth Mother—Gaia.

This scientific theory suggests that all the earth's lands, oceans, atmosphere, and living matter are completely and complexly integrated into a single system which, left on its own, maintains its climatic, biological, geological, and chemical conditions in perpetual equilibrium. As P. H. Liotta and Allan W. Shearer explain in their work, *Gaia's Revenge*:

> Over time, different versions of the hypothesis emerged, some that maximally stated that biota influence the larger environment, others that maximally stated biota manipulate the environment to produce the best conditions for life.

> Somewhere in the middle is the position that planetary homeostasis—the particular balance of conditions that regulate temperature and atmospheric composition that allows life to exist—is provided *by* the biosphere, but not *for* the biosphere. That is, although life as a whole has not intentionally engineered the planet for its own benefit, life does, nonetheless, contribute to the maintenance of this extraordinary circumstance.[1]

In other words, without interference, particularly the interference of human beings, the earth would remain in perfect balance. At first glance, it's a shocking idea. As Lovelock writes:

> You may find it hard to swallow the notion that anything as large and apparently inanimate as the Earth is alive. Surely, you may say, the Earth is almost wholly rock, and nearly all incandescent with heat. The difficulty can be lessened if you let the image of a giant redwood tree enter your mind. The tree undoubtedly is alive, yet 99 percent of it is dead. The great tree is an ancient spire of dead wood, made of lignin and cellulose by the ancestors of the thin layer of living cells which constitute its bark. How like the Earth, and more so when we realize that many of the atoms of the rocks far down into the magma were once part of the ancestral life of which we all have come.[2]

But there is a small problem. If you consider the entire earth as a single and unique entity capable of maintaining an internal and integral balance, it is a relatively easy jump to see it as a cohesive unity expressing life in the same way that a tree is said to be alive and then, in another mental skip, attributing some kind of sentience to it—believing that the earth is somehow capable of a collective consciousness. From there, it is not a huge leap to make the planet responsible for its own creation, in essence, assigning it divinity. (Thus returning to the original divine being of mythology—Gaia.) This is precisely what many are trying to do: make the incredibly complex Creation that is our world into the Creator in and of itself.

The Earth: God's Gift

Such an idea is in direct opposition to Judeo-Christian teaching which clearly holds, according to the opening words of Genesis, that "in the beginning, when God created the heavens and the earth, the earth was a formless wasteland, and darkness covered the abyss, while a mighty wind swept over the waters." Thus, the earth must be viewed as a product of God's Creation, not as a Creator itself. In other words, it is a mistake to think that the earth is somehow capable of producing and sustaining itself apart from God. The Holy See has increasingly called attention to the fallacy of seeing nature as having independent creative powers, pointing out that such radical environmentalism that sees the earth and nature as a divine reality reduces or eliminates the importance of human life.

At a Vatican symposium in 2005 on "Original Sin: An Interdisciplinary Perspective," Joan Andreu Rocha Scarpetta, professor of theology of religions at the Regina Apostolorum Pontifical University, pointed out, "The sin in contemporary radical environmentalism consists in divinizing nature, in suffocating the importance of the human being as custodian of

Creation, and in forgetting God as author of man's natural surroundings." Professor Rocha went on to say, "Contemporary radical environmentalism has forgotten divine transcendence; it has placed man on the same level or below nature" and, in forgetting the created character of nature, "has given it a magical, almost divine value." He added that "sin manifests itself when the relationship between God-the-creator, man-custodian, and created nature is unbalanced. . . . When God's creative action is forgotten, man is placed at the same level as the rest of Creation, or a transcendent or magical character is attributed to created nature."[3]

Pope Benedict, while not specifically referring to the fallacy of considering the earth as divine, has emphasized that the earth is neither equal to nor superior to humanity, but is, in fact, God's gift to mankind. On World Peace Day 2007, he said:

> In his Encyclical Letter *Centesimus Annus*, Pope John Paul II wrote: "Not only has God given the earth to man, who must use it with respect for the original good purpose for which it was given to him, but man too is God's gift to man. He must therefore respect the natural and moral structure with which he has been endowed." By responding to this charge, entrusted to them by the Creator, men and women can join in bringing about a world of peace. Alongside the ecology of nature, there exists what can be called a "human" ecology, which in turn demands a "social" ecology. All this means that humanity, if it truly desires peace, must be increasingly conscious of the links between natural ecology, or respect for nature, and human ecology. Experience shows that *disregard for the environment always harms*

> *human coexistence*, and vice versa. It becomes more and more evident that there is an inseparable link between peace with Creation and peace among men. Both of these presuppose peace with God. The poem-prayer of Saint Francis, known as "the Canticle of Brother Sun," is a wonderful and ever timely example of this multifaceted ecology of peace.[4]

Given that nature is not a sacred or divine reality removed from human intervention, the Holy See points out that human intervention that modifies some characteristics of living things is not wrong, as long as it respects their place in nature. As Cardinal Renato Martino, president of the Pontifical Council for Justice and Peace, said at a conference on climate change and development, "Nature is for the human person and the human person is for God. . . . In considering the problems associated with climate change, one must look to the social doctrine of the Church, [which] neither supports the absolutization of nature, nor the reduction of nature to a mere instrument. . . . Nature is not an absolute, but a wealth that is placed in the person's responsible and prudent hands."

A Home for the Human Family

Pope Benedict understands that humanity will modify the earth in some way or other, merely by living on it. That modification is not wrong, so long as it is done with "creativity and responsibility." On World Peace Day, 2008, he explained:

> The family needs a home, a fit environment in which to develop its proper relationships. *For the human family, this home is the earth,* the

environment that God the Creator has given us to inhabit with creativity and responsibility. We need to care for the environment: it has been entrusted to men and women to be protected and cultivated with responsible freedom, with the good of all as a constant guiding criterion. Human beings, obviously, are of supreme worth vis-à-vis Creation as a whole. Respecting the environment does not mean considering material or animal nature more important than man. Rather, it means not selfishly considering nature to be at the complete disposal of our own interests, for future generations also have the right to reap its benefits and to exhibit towards nature the same responsible freedom that we claim for ourselves. Nor must we overlook the poor, who are excluded in many cases from the goods of Creation destined for all. Humanity today is rightly concerned about the ecological balance of tomorrow. It is important for assessments in this regard to be carried out prudently, in dialogue with experts and people of wisdom, uninhibited by ideological pressure to draw hasty conclusions, and above all with the aim of reaching agreement on a model of sustainable development capable of ensuring the well-being of all while respecting environmental balances.[5]

At the 2005 congress on "Ethics and the Environment," Legionary Father Paolo Scarafoni, rector of the European University of Rome, explained that humanity, being both free and intelligent, is called to help develop the created world, saying that although people do make errors, they can, with the help of God's grace, do good as well.[6] At that same conference, Cardinal Renato Martino said that ecological problems must be considered ethical problems as well and that "people's actions in the created world should not be considered merely as an exercise of their technical capacity to deal with matters."[7] Likewise, Bishop Giampaolo Crepaldi noted that the *Compendium* "steers a middle course between the twin errors of either seeing nature in absolute terms or reducing it to a mere instrument. Nature has been placed in the hands of mankind, but should be used responsibly and prudently." Bishop Crepaldi added that human begins do not have absolute dominion over Creation, but our actions should be "guided by a combination of conservation and development, and people should realize that the created goods of this world are destined for the use of all."[8]

Pope Benedict's vision of humanity's role in and toward the environment draws on and contributes to the vision given in the *Compendium*. In that document, the Magisterium points out, "In his public ministry, Jesus makes use of natural elements. Not only is he a knowledgeable interpreter of nature, speaking of it in images and parables, but he also dominates it (cf. the episode of the calming of the storm in Mt 14:22–33; Mk 6:45–52; Lk 8:22–25; Jn 6:16–21). The Lord puts nature at the service of his plan of Redemption" (*Compendium*, 453). Following the Lord's example, we too can use, though not abuse, nature. The *Compendium* further explains:

> Nature is not a sacred or divine reality that man must leave alone. Rather, it is a gift offered by the Creator to the human community, entrusted to the intelligence and moral responsibility of men and women. For this reason the human person does not commit an illicit act when, out of respect for the order, beauty, and usefulness of individual living beings and their function in the ecosystem,

he intervenes by modifying some of their characteristics or properties. Human interventions that
damage living beings or the natural environment
deserve condemnation, while those that improve
them are praiseworthy. The acceptability of the
use of biological and biogenetic techniques is
only one part of the ethical problem: as with
every human behavior, it is also necessary to
evaluate accurately the real benefits as well as the
possible consequences in terms of risks. In the
realm of technological-scientific interventions
that have forceful and widespread impact on living organisms, with the possibility of significant
long-term repercussions, it is unacceptable to act
lightly or irresponsibly. (*Compendium*, 473)

Modifying Nature

So what sort of environmental modifications are
acceptable? The Vatican has never directly spelled
out what is meant by being "done within the context
of a respect for [nature's] order and beauty, and taking
into consideration the utility of every creature." It
thus leaves room for our own rational reflection on
particular cases of intervention into nature. Although
the morality of some cases may be relatively easy to
determine, others can be quite complex. We can see
this by considering one particular example of human
intervention into nature: the use of river dams.

At first glance, the use of river dams would seem
to be an obvious example of a positive intervention
into nature. Humans have been damming rivers for at
least five thousand years. The earliest site is north of
what is now Amman, Jordan, and the oldest surviving
dam is the Quatinah barrage in modern-day Syria,

which dates back to about 1310 BC. Dams provide flood control, regulate water levels, allow for controlled irrigation and better navigation, as well as, in modern times, providing hydroelectrical power. However, they also raise concerns about the relocation of people, loss of archaeological and cultural heritage sites, as well as the indisputable impact to the local ecosystem.

Consider, for example, the Three Gorges Dam on the Yangtze River in China. Completed in October 2008, the hydroelectrical power produced by the dam will potentially reduce coal use by 31 million tons per year, cutting the emission into the atmosphere of 100 million tons of greenhouse gas, millions of tons of dust, 1 million tons of sulfur dioxide, 370 thousand tons of nitric oxide, 10 thousand tons of carbon monoxide, and a significant amount of mercury. The dam will also provide substantial protection against flooding ,which has been a major problem in that area of China (1998 floods in the area left 4,000 dead and 14 million homeless and cost $24 billion in economic loss).[9]

On the other hand, with the building of the dam, 1.24 million people from 13 cities, 140 towns, and 1,300 villages had to be relocated, and 1,600 factories and abandoned mines have been submerged, creating toxic hazards for the people and animals who depend on the river for survival. In addition, the quality of water in the Yangtze is deteriorating because the 265 billion gallons of raw sewage dumped into the river annually is being backed up by the dam. Also worthy of note are the loss of habitat for the endangered Siberian Crane, the virtual extinction of the Baiji Yangtze river dolphin, and the permanent destruction of as many as 1,300 known archaeological sites.[10] Clearly this is the sort of environmental modification that the Vatican and Pope Benedict are saying must be undertaken with care and respect for the natural order in order to balance the gains and losses.

Here again, Pope Benedict does more than just talk about the issues; he puts his beliefs in action. During the planning of World Youth Day 2008, the first under his pontificate, special emphasis was placed on making sure that the impact of the many pilgrims would be lessened as much as possible, with the result that the Australian event was the "greenest" Youth Day ever. Zenit news agency reported that Auxiliary Bishop Anthony Fisher of Sydney said that one goal was to "leave the environment better off at the end," adding, "On a per capita basis this group will be far and away the lowest-polluting crowd for an event in Sydney. They're using the very minimum of energy and are maximizing the use of recyclable and biodegradable product."[11] For example, attendees were given reusable batteries in the flashlights provided for them, and were also given a three-minute timer for their showers to minimize water use. In addition, a huge tree-planting program was a carbon-offset for those traveling to Australia by plane.

WHAT

PRICE

PROGRESS?

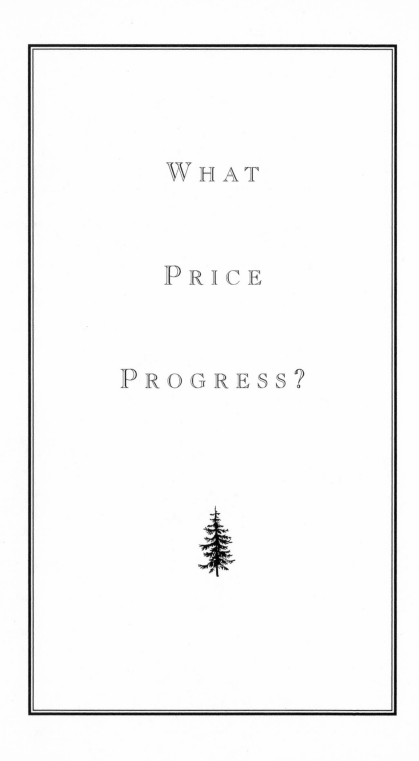

ECOLOGICAL QUESTIONS HIGHLIGHT THE
NEED TO ACHIEVE A GREATER HARMONY
BOTH BETWEEN MEASURES DESIGNED TO
PROMOTE ECONOMIC DEVELOPMENT AND
THOSE DIRECTED TO PRESERVING THE
ECOLOGY, AND BETWEEN NATIONAL AND
INTERNATIONAL POLICIES. **ECONOMIC
DEVELOPMENT, MOREOVER, NEEDS TO
TAKE INTO CONSIDERATION THE
INTEGRITY AND RHYTHM OF NATURE,
BECAUSE NATURAL RESOURCES ARE LIM-
ITED.** AND ALL ECONOMIC ACTIVITY THAT
USES NATURAL RESOURCES SHOULD ALSO
INCLUDE THE COSTS OF SAFEGUARDING
THE ENVIRONMENT INTO THE CALCULA-
TIONS OF THE OVERALL COSTS OF ITS
ACTIVITY.

I n his address to the U.N., Holy See representative Celestino Migliore set out the message that underlies this sixth commandment for the environment:

> It is often said that we have to defend the environment. The term "defense" could mislead us to see a conflict between the environment and the human being. In this forum, we speak of "protection" or "safeguarding." Indeed, in this case, protection encompasses more than defense. It implies a positive vision of the human being, meaning that the person is considered not a nuisance or a threat to the environment, but as its steward. In this sense, not only is there no opposition between the human being and the environment, but there is an established and inseparable alliance, in which the environment essentially conditions the human being's existence and development, while the latter perfects and ennobles the environment by his creative activity.[1]

Which brings us to a fundamental point. We all agree that it's important, but what does it cost to "safeguard the environment"? The truth is nobody really knows. We know what it costs to clean up a mess like the Valdez oil spill in Alaska (more than 2.1 billion dollars),[2] and environmental groups have created staggeringly complicated protocol for trying to predict future cleanup costs, but the fact remains that we are better at hindsight than foresight when it comes to cost and ecology. One thing seems apparent, however. It will cost less to protect the environment than to try to salvage it. For example, Nat Keohane, Ph.D., director of economic policy and analysis for the Environmental Defense Fund, says that the cost of capping global warming pollution over the next two decades is almost "too small to measure."[3]

Which is precisely why Pope Benedict has focused attention on the matter of the price of progress. As he said to the Seventh Symposium on Religion, Science, and the Environment:

> Preservation of the environment, promotion of sustainable development and particular attention to climate change are matters of grave concern for the entire human family. No nation or business sector can ignore the ethical implications present in all economic and social development. With increasing clarity scientific research demonstrates that the impact of human actions in any one place or region can have worldwide effects. The consequences of disregard for the environment cannot be limited to an immediate area or populace because they always harm human coexistence, and thus betray human dignity and violate the rights of citizens who desire to live in a safe environment.[4]

Sustainable Development

Of all the topics addressed by the Commandments for the Environment, this may be the most delicate and complex. The key here is the issue of economic development versus environmental concerns, especially as it relates to emerging nations. Developed nations have used (and often overused) their natural resources to reach their current levels of economic development. Third World nations in particular, who have resources the world desires, such as timber from the rainforests, do not believe it is fair that they should have to restrict the use of resources that would increase their economic development simply because other nations have exploited and destroyed those same resources in the process of becoming wealthy. Conversely, rich nations are often tempted to exploit the natural wealth of developing nations to increase their own wealth. Both are improper uses of the world's limited resources. As Benedict said in a message sent in his name in 2007 to the annual symposium known as the Social Weeks of France, "The richest nations must not unduly exploit the resources of developing nations without giving into the hands of the latter the incomes derived from their land and below ground resources."[5]

The *Compendium* makes this responsibility clear:

> An economy respectful of the environment will not have the maximization of profits as its only objective, because environmental protection cannot be assured solely on the basis of financial calculations of costs and benefits. The environment is one of those goods that cannot be adequately safeguarded or promoted by market forces. Every country, in particular developed countries, must be aware of the urgent obligation to reconsider the way that natural goods are being used. Seeking innovative ways to reduce the environmental impact of production and consumption of goods should be effectively encouraged. (*Compendium*, 470)

Pope Benedict expressed much the same thought when he said:

While it is true that industrializing countries are not morally free to repeat the past errors of others, by recklessly continuing to damage the environment, it is also the case that highly industrialized countries must share "clean-technologies" and ensure that their own markets do not sustain demand for goods whose very production contributes to the proliferation of pollution. Mutual interdependence between nations' economic and social activities demands international solidarity, cooperation and ongoing educational efforts.[6]

But the Holy See is well aware that the *how* of creating sustainable development lies not with theologians, but with scientists. As Msgr. Renato Martino said at the World Summit on sustainable development in 2002,

The Holy See will not attempt to add to the significant technical discourse underway regarding sustainable development. Nevertheless, the Holy See is deeply committed to the values that inspire actions and decisions regarding sustainable development, since the deliberations that take place have a particular historical context and lead directly to concepts of the person, society and the common good.[7]

Perhaps the clearest statement on those values came from Benedict's representative Celestino Migliore in the Vatican's address to the U.N. on climate change in May 2007:

Thus, in order to address the double challenge of climate change and the need for ever greater energy resources, we will have to change our present model from one of the heedless pursuit of economic growth in the name of development, toward a model which heeds the consequences of its actions and is more respectful toward the creation we hold in common, coupled with an integral human development for present and future generations.

The complexity of the promotion of sustainable development is evident to all; there are, however, certain underlying principles which can direct research toward adequate and lasting solutions. Humanity must become increasingly conscious of the links between natural ecology, or respect for nature, and human ecology. Experience shows that disregard for the environment harms human coexistence, while at the same time it becomes clearer that there is a positive link to be made between peace with creation and peace among nations. . . .

Recently, we have heard of economies that have managed to grow while actually reducing their consumption of energy. Surely this success holds out hope that our current economic model does not always oblige us to use more and more energy in order to grow. Economic growth does not have to mean greater consumption. From the standpoint of a sustainable economy, it does however mean that we will need technology, ingenuity, determined political will and common sense. Importantly, it will also demand technology transfer to developing countries, to the benefit of the entire global community. . . .

Worldwide, unprecedented ecological changes are already taking place and none of us can foresee fully the consequences of man's industrial activity over the recent centuries. Remedies are not beyond our ingenuity, but we should however be careful not to choose a path that will make things worse, especially for the poor. We cannot simply uninvent the modern world, but there is still time to use technology and education to promote universally sustainable development before it is too late.[8]

Limited Natural Resources

But sustainable development is not the only aspect of this commandment. The second dimension focuses not on economics as much as on the economy, that is, the very nature of natural resources themselves. Obviously, natural resources are not unlimited. For example, some experts believe the world's oil will run out by 2030 unless new reserves are discovered,[9] and the Brazilian rainforest, which the *Compendium* calls "one of the world's most precious natural regions because of its biodiversity," is being destroyed at the rate of nearly 8,000 hectares per year.[10]

Pope Benedict undoubtedly had such facts in mind when he addressed the Director General of the Food and Agriculture Organization, saying, "The order of creation demands that priority be given to those human activities that do not cause irreversible damage to nature, but which instead are woven into the social, cultural and religious fabric of the different communities. In this way, a sober balance is achieved between consumption and the sustainability of resources."[11]

The *Compendium* further elucidates the importance of preserving the integrity of nature by pointing out:

> The present rhythm of exploitation is seriously compromising the availability of some natural

resources for both the present and the future. Solutions to the ecological problem require that economic activity respect the environment to a greater degree, reconciling the needs of economic development with those of environmental protection. Every economic activity making use of natural resources must also be concerned with safeguarding the environment and should foresee the costs involved, which are "an essential element of the actual cost of economic activity." In this context, one considers relations between human activity and climate change which, given their extreme complexity, must be opportunely and constantly monitored at the scientific, political and juridical, national and international levels. The climate is a good that must be protected and reminds consumers and those engaged in industrial activity to develop a greater sense of responsibility for their behavior. (*Compendium*, 470)

This need for a sense of accountability was further stressed by Vatican representative Celestino Migliore:

In a world so interconnected as today, we are witnessing the rapid expansion of a series of challenges in many areas of human life, from food crisis to financial turmoil. Such crises have revealed the limited national resources and capacities to deal with them adequately, and the increasing need for collective action by the international community . . . it should be borne in mind that the environmental question cannot be considered separately from other issues, like energy and economy, peace and justice, national interests and international solidarity. It is not difficult to perceive how issues of environmental protection, models of development, social equity and shared responsibility to care for the environment are inextricably linked.[12]

Benedict himself tucked this same message of the need for cooperation in an increasingly interconnected world into his December 2008 welcome to the new ambassador of Malawi to the Vatican:

> [There is an] urgent need for unity and cooperation in facing the challenges of the future and ensuring sound and integral development for [the world's] people. This demands wise and far-sighted policies, the prudent stewardship of resources, and a resolve to curb corruption and injustice, as well as to promote civic responsibility and fraternal solidarity at every level of society. In a special way, political leaders must have a deep sense of their duty to advance the common good, and thus be firmly committed to dialogue and readiness to transcend particular interests in the service of the whole body politic. . . . Economically and ethically sound models of development must include a specific commitment to respect the natural environment, which is a treasure entrusted to all humanity to be responsibly cultivated and protected for the good of future generations.[13]

As much as Pope Benedict appreciates the role of government and science in helping to preserve the earth, and as much as he realizes that economic development and protection of the environment must work together, his unique contribution to the subject comes from his conviction that Creation and the Creator are intrinsically and irrevocably linked. As we have already observed in earlier chapters, underlying all of Pope Benedict XVI's statements is the fundamental premise that without an understanding that all life on the planet begins and ends with God, anything we do to try to save the earth will ultimately be futile. For Benedict, protecting the environment is, at its deepest level, about learning to be responsible stewards of the Creation that the Creator has given into our charge until the fullness of time is completed.

FLOWING

LIKE

A RIVER

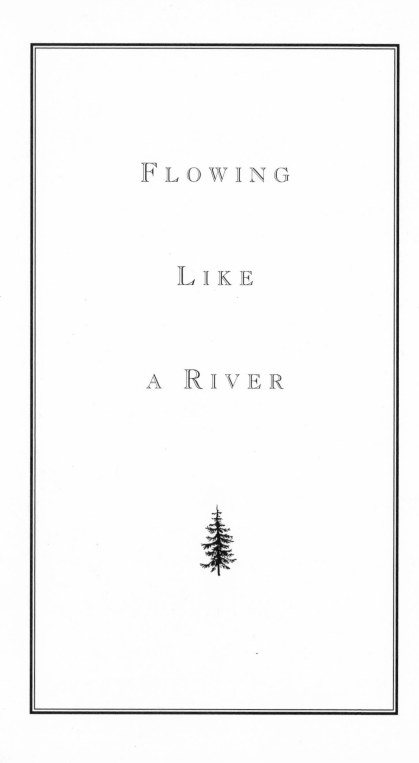

CONCERN FOR THE ENVIRONMENT MEANS
THAT WE SHOULD ACTIVELY WORK FOR THE
INTEGRAL DEVELOPMENT OF THE POOREST
REGIONS. **THE GOODS OF THIS WORLD
HAVE BEEN CREATED BY GOD TO BE
WISELY USED BY ALL. THESE GOODS
SHOULD BE SHARED, IN A JUST AND
CHARITABLE MANNER.** THE PRINCIPLE OF
THE UNIVERSAL DESTINY OF GOODS OFFERS
A FUNDAMENTAL ORIENTATION TO DEAL
WITH THE COMPLEX RELATIONSHIP
BETWEEN ECOLOGY AND POVERTY.

Ever since Jesus himself said, "Blessed are the poor" (Mt 5:3), the Catholic Church has taken a special interest in caring for the most needy. Passages of the New Testament, including Acts 4:32–35, 1 Corinthians 16:1, and Galatians 2:10, indicate the high level of concern for the poor in the nascent church. The story of St. Lawrence, who lived in the third century, is a good example of the emphasis the Church has placed on the poor. Lawrence was given three days to turn over the riches of the Church to the Roman prefect. He gave away as much as he could to avoid having it seized by the authorities, and on the third day he arrived before the court as ordered. When the prefect demanded the wealth, Lawrence showed him the poor, the crippled, the blind, and the suffering, saying these were the true treasures of the Church. Needless to say, his attitude did not sit well with the establishment, and he was martyred. However, his story is one especially compelling example of the Church's consistent care for the poor.

Pope Benedict addressed this point in his message for the World Day of Peace 2009:

> The Church's social teaching has always been concerned with the poor. At the time of the Encyclical Letter *Rerum Novarum*, the poor were identified mainly as the workers in the new industrial society; in the social Magisterium of Pius XI, Pius XII, John XXIII, Paul VI, and John

Paul II, new forms of poverty were gradually explored, as the scope of the social question widened to reach global proportions. This expansion of the social question to the worldwide scale has to be considered not just as a quantitative extension, but also as a qualitative growth in the understanding of man and the needs of the human family.

For this reason, while attentively following the current phenomena of globalization and their impact on human poverty, the Church points out the new aspects of the social question, not only in their breadth but also in their depth, insofar as they concern man's identity and his relationship with God. These principles of social teaching tend to clarify the links between poverty and globalization and they help to guide action towards the building of peace. Among these principles, it is timely to recall in particular the "preferential love for the poor," in the light of the primacy of charity, which is attested throughout Christian tradition, beginning with that of the early Church.[1]

As Benedict points out, this "preferential option for the poor" has taken on a new dimension as globalization has heightened the impact of the environmental crisis facing the entire world. While all nations and all peoples are involved, the poor are disproportionately affected when natural resources are squandered and the environment plundered.

Archbishop Fernando Filoni, representative of the Vatican Secretary of State, emphasized this when he spoke on behalf of Pope Benedict in 2007 at the Social Weeks of France:

Men's fears today are multiple: exhaustion of the resources of the planet, rapid melting of the ice-caps, elevation in greenhouse emissions, increase in natural disasters, excessive CO_2 emissions. These are some of the alarm bells which invite us to take a moral stand in favor of the earth. Once again, it will be the poorest countries which will have to undergo the most serious consequences of the attitude of the industrialized world and the sometimes excessive confidence given to scientific progress and technique.

The Creator gave man his Spirit, so that, in a reasoned manner, we can unceasingly make projects which will allow a better natural allocation of resources and goods of the earth, for a measured use of forests and biological reserves. . . . One of the elementary principles of justice and equity concerns the universal destiny of the goods of the earth.[2]

The Universal Destination of Goods

Much of the Seventh Commandment for the Environment rests on the concept of "universal destination of goods." In short, this concept means that the world and all its bounty has been created for the good of all human beings. Every person is entitled to enough food to eat, clean water to drink, clothing, housing, and sufficient other material possessions to live in dignity. When individuals or nations take more than their share and prevent others from having access to these material commodities, the "universal destination of goods" is thwarted. As the *Compendium* explains, "[The goods of the earth] must be shared equitably, in accordance with justice and charity.

This is essentially a question of preventing the injustice of hoarding resources: greediness, be it individual or collective, is contrary to the order of Creation" (*Compendium*, 481). The document goes on to explain that "the present environmental crisis affects those who are poorest in a particular way, whether they live in those lands subject to erosion and desertification, are involved in armed conflicts or subject to forced immigration, or because they do not have the economic and technological means to protect themselves from other calamities" (*Compendium*, 482).

It is not that God's provision is insufficient for the world. Jesus said that he came to give us abundant life, which, in addition to spiritual riches, presumably means adequate material possessions for the well-being of all peoples. As Pope Benedict has said, "The earth, in fact, can produce enough to nourish all its inhabitants, on the condition that the rich countries do not keep for themselves what belongs to all."[3] Once again, Pope Benedict points out that the greed and selfishness that result in some having more than they can possibly use while others do not have enough to survive underlies the poverty that plagues so much of the world. Consider that half the world's population—nearly three billion people—lives on an average of $500 a year. To put this in perspective, Bill Gates earns $500 every second. By himself, Gates is wealthier than the seventy poorest nations on earth.[4]

A Vulnerable Population

The inequitable distribution of resources has an impact beyond its effect on the relative standards of living of the rich and the poor. As the *Compendium* points out, the poor bear the greater brunt of ecological and environmental upheavals. Poor nations and sectors of society are particularly vulnerable to the adverse consequences of climate change due to lesser resources and capacity to mitigate their effects and adapt to altered surroundings.

It's not just man-created problems like Chernobyl that concern the Vatican when it comes to the needs of the poor. Natural disasters, too, are part of the equation. Indeed, "natural disasters are not solely caused by nature, but also by an inconsiderate use and consumption of the earth's resources."[5] We need look no further than the residents of New Orleans who were displaced by Hurricane Katrina to realize that even in the wealthiest nation on earth, those who live in poverty are the ones most harmed by natural disasters because they often lack the ability to get out of the path of the disaster as well as the resources to rebuild afterward.

At the fourth World Water Forum held in Mexico City in 2006, the Pontifical Council for Justice and Peace expanded on this point:

> The world's population should share equitably in the benefits of modern technological means for early disaster risk assessments. Disaster risk assessment is an integral component of development plans and poverty eradication programs, and ways need to be found to break the vicious circle between poverty, environmental degradation, and lack of preparation that turns natural hazards into disasters that destroy development gains.
>
> Poor countries, especially, should be encouraged, with the help of the richer ones, to invest

in mitigation measures to reduce the consequences of floods and droughts. For example,
water reserves to face periods of drought should
be created. But all such initiatives should be
implemented with an active involvement of the
local communities. They should be accurately
informed of the impacts on the environment and
on their lives of any infrastructure built with the
aim of reducing vulnerability to natural disasters.
This is, indeed, an important element which contributes to the sustainable development of a
country. The required large-scale nature of such
activity will necessitate the provision of addition-
al resources by developed countries while not
reducing the small and medium projects funded
in the water sector.[6]

A Vital Resource

Which brings us to one of the environmental concerns that appears to trouble Pope Benedict the
most—the availability of clean, potable water. Not long
after his investiture as pontiff, the first-ever Working
Group on Water and the Environment was sponsored
by the Pontifical Academy of Sciences. The scientists
and ethicists who met at the Vatican in November
2005 examined the conservation of water and its equitable distribution, as well as its impact on world politics as resources become increasingly scarce.[7] This
concern for water carried over to the Vatican's partici-
pation in the Fourth World Water Forum in Mexico
City. In its contribution to the forum, quoted above,
the Vatican eloquently expressed the need for an adequate water supply for all persons:

Water is a natural resource vital for the survival of humanity and all species on earth. As a good of Creation, water is destined for all human beings and their communities. God intended the earth and all it contains for the use of all, so that all created things would be shared fairly by humankind under the guidance of justice tempered by charity.

Human beings, and the communities in which they live, cannot do without water since it corresponds to their primary needs and constitutes a basic condition of their existence. All depend upon the fate of water. Access to safe water and sanitation is indispensable for the life and full development of all human beings and communities in the world.[8]

This statement is in agreement with Msgr. Renato R. Martino's statement to the Third World Water Forum in Kyoto in 2003:

Water is a universal common good, a common good of the entire human family. Its benefits are meant for all and not only for those who live in countries where water is abundant, well managed, and well distributed. This natural resource must be equitably at the disposal of the entire human family. The few, with the means to control, cannot destroy or exhaust this resource, which is destined for the use of all. . . .

Water plays a central and critical role in all aspects of life—in the national environment, in our economies, in food security, in production, in politics. Water has indeed a special significance for the great religions. The inadequacy in the supply and access to water has only recently taken center stage in global reflection as a serious and threatening phenomenon. Communities and individuals can exist even for substantial periods without many essential goods. The human being, however, can survive only a few days without clean, safe drinking water.

Many people living in poverty, particularly in the developing countries, daily face enormous hardship because water supplies are neither sufficient nor safe. Women bear a disproportionate hardship. For water users living in poverty this is rapidly becoming an issue crucial for life and, in the broad sense of the concept, *a right to life issue.*[9]

Finally, in his historic visit to Turkey in December 2006, in a homily focused on Christ, our river of living water, Benedict also added an environmental message that echoes the sentiments expressed above, saying, "In a world where men are so loath to share the earth's goods . . . there is a dramatic shortage of water, the good so precious for the life of the body."[10]

An Urgent Need

Those who live in countries where clean water is readily available at the flick of a tap cannot fully appreciate the importance of this resource. Consider for a moment:

- 1.1 million people in developing countries do not have adequate access to water, and 2.6 billion lack basic sanitation.

- Almost two in three people who do not have access to clean water survive on less than $2 a day, with one in three living on less than $1 a day.

- Access to piped water into the household averages about 85 percent for the wealthiest 20 percent of the population, compared with 25 percent for the poorest 20 percent.

- 1.8 billion people who have access to a water source within 1 kilometer, but not in their house or yard, consume around 5 gallons per day. The highest average water use in the world is in the U.S., at 158 gallons per day.

- Some 1.8 million children die each year from diarrhea.

- Close to half of all people in developing countries suffer from a health problem caused by water and sanitation deficits.[11]

- 400 million children (1 in 5 from the developing world) have no access to safe water; 1.4 million children will die each year from lack of access to safe drinking water and adequate sanitation.[12]

- 12 percent of the world's population uses 85 percent of its water.[13]

To bring the statistics to a more comprehensible level—in the fall of 2008, more than 12,000 people in Zimbabwe had contracted cholera because of unclean water. Even Harare, the capital, had no running water, and Zimbabweans were forced to dig holes, often near latrines or polluted rivers, in the hopes of finding some water. Cholera is a widely contagious and often fatal disease that is highly curable, but because the government could not (or would not) buy chemicals to treat the water and the country lacked both the drugs and doctors to treat the sick, the death rate reached epidemic proportions.[14] Bodies were literally stacking up for want of antibiotics and purifying chemicals that cost mere pennies, while consumers in nations with potable tap water spend

more than $100 billion annually for bottled water.
What is most shocking is that, according to the Earth
Policy Institute, for a fraction of that $100 billion,
everyone on the planet could have safe drinking
water and proper sanitation.[15]

The Dignity of the Human Person

For Pope Benedict, the complex global issues that
link environmental concerns and poverty come down
to one thing—the importance and centrality of the
dignity of the human person, regardless of wealth or
stature. As the *Compendium* states:

> The close link that exists between the develop-
> ment of the poorest countries, demographic
> changes and a sustainable use of the environ-
> ment must not become a pretext for political and
> economic choices that are at variance with the
> dignity of the human person. In developed coun-
> tries there is a drop in the birth-rates, with reper-
> cussions on the aging of the population, unable
> even to renew itself biologically. The situation is
> different in the developing countries where
> demographic changes are increasing. Although it
> is true that an uneven distribution of the popula-
> tion and of available resources creates obstacles
> to development and a sustainable use of the envi-
> ronment, it must nonetheless be recognized that
> demographic growth is fully compatible with an
> integral and shared development. There is wide-
> spread agreement that a population policy is
> only one part of an overall development strategy.
> Accordingly, it is important that any discussion
> of population policies should keep in mind the
> actual and projected development of nations and
> regions. At the same time, it is impossible to

leave out of account the very nature of what is meant by the term "development." All development worthy of the name must be integral, that is, it must be directed to the true good of every person and of the whole person. (*Compendium*, 483)

Pope Benedict himself echoed these words in his Message for World Peace Day 2009:

In the Encyclical Letter *Centesimus Annus*, John Paul II warned of the need to "abandon a mentality in which the poor—as individuals and as peoples—are considered a burden, as irksome intruders trying to consume what others have produced." The poor, he wrote, "ask for the right to share in enjoying material goods and to make good use of their capacity for work, thus creating a world that is more just and prosperous for all." In today's globalized world, it is increasingly evident that peace can be built only if everyone is assured the possibility of reasonable growth: sooner or later, the distortions produced by unjust systems have to be paid for by everyone. It is utterly foolish to build a luxury home in the midst of desert or decay. Globalization on its own is incapable of building peace, and in many cases, it actually creates divisions and conflicts. If anything it points to a need: to be oriented towards a goal of profound solidarity that seeks the good of each and all. In this sense, globalization should be seen as a good opportunity to achieve something important in the fight against poverty, and to place at the disposal of justice and peace resources which were scarcely conceivable previously.[16]

WE'RE ALL

IN THE

SAME BOAT

COLLABORATION, BY MEANS OF WORLD-WIDE AGREEMENTS, BACKED UP BY INTERNATIONAL LAW, IS NECESSARY TO PROTECT THE ENVIRONMENT. RESPONSIBILITY TOWARD THE ENVIRONMENT NEEDS TO BE IMPLEMENTED IN AN ADEQUATE WAY AT THE JURIDICAL LEVEL. THESE LAWS AND AGREEMENTS SHOULD BE GUIDED BY THE DEMANDS OF THE COMMON GOOD.

ere's a quick quiz. What's the difference between the Holy See, the Vatican, and the Pope?

For most people, the terms are often more or less interchangeable. When we use any of them, we generally are thinking of the Catholic Church and its leadership. However, the three aren't the same at all. The Holy See is the sovereign spiritual and diplomatic authority exercised by the Pope; it also includes various offices, especially the tribunals and congregations assisting the Pope in the government of the Church. The Vatican, officially the State of Vatican City, is a 110-acre walled in city-state within Rome; it is the political entity and territory in which the Holy See is located and that guarantees the Holy See's independence. The Pope is the man who is the head of the Catholic Church. The distinctions are important because, while Pope Benedict (who lives in the Vatican) has made statements about the importance of international agreements on ecological issues, it is the Holy See that participates in diplomatic activity throughout the world, and it is essentially the Holy See that implements this Eighth Commandment for the Environment.

So let's take a quick look at these three entities.

The Pope is the Bishop of Rome, the leader of the Roman Catholic Church and the head of state of the independent sovereign State of Vatican City. His office is called the papacy. Benedict XVI is the two-hundred-sixty-fifth in a long line of popes that started with Peter.

The Vatican is a city-state that came into existence in 1929 under the terms of the Lateran Treaty with Italy. The agreements included a political treaty that created the state of Vatican City and guaranteed full and independent sovereignty to the Holy See. The Vatican consists of approximately 110 acres completely encircled by the city of Rome and approximately 825 citizens. The Vatican has its own heliport and a railway spur, as well as an independent telephone system. Its post office is considered one of the most efficient in the world, and its pharmacy is the busiest in the world, serving two thousand customers per day.[1] Industries include banking and finance as well as printing and production of coins, medals, postage stamps, and mosaics. The official radio station, Vatican Radio, is one of the most influential in Europe. The semi-official newspaper, *L'Osservatore Romano*, is published daily in Italian and weekly in English, Spanish, Portuguese, German, Malayalam (an Indian language), and French. Approximately three thousand people work at Vatican City.[2]

Sometimes "The Vatican" is used to refer to St. Peter's, that is, the Basilica of St. Peter's in the Vatican. The burial place of St. Peter and symbol of the Catholic Church, St. Peter's is not the official ecclesiastical seat of the Pope. That honor belongs to the Basilica of St. John Lateran, which is the oldest and first major basilica of Rome and is called the "ecumenical mother church."

The Holy See, the government of the Catholic Church, operates from the independent territory of Vatican City state. As a formal entity under international law, it maintains diplomatic relations with 177 nations as well as special relations with the Russian Federation and the Organization for the Liberation of Palestine.[3]

The Holy See's existence as a temporal state has waxed and waned over the centuries. From the eighth to the mid-nineteenth century, the Papal States ruled a wide swath of central Italy, but in 1870 Victor Emmanuel named Rome the capital of Italy and ended papal control. Pope Pius IX and his successors argued over these actions, and in 1929 the Italian Government and the Holy See signed three agreements which created the current arrangement. The agreements included:

ɶ a treaty recognizing the independence and sovereignty of the Holy See and creating the State of Vatican City;

ɶ a concordat defining the relations between the government and the church within Italy;

ɶ and a financial convention providing the Holy See with compensation for its losses in 1870.[4]

So how does the Pope, as both head of state and as moral leader for the world's Catholic population, interact with the government of the Holy See?

The internal administration of Vatican City is in the hands of the Pontifical Commission for the State of Vatican City. The Pope rules through the Roman Curia and the Papal Civil Service. The Curia consists of the Secretariat of State, nine congregations, three tribunals, eleven pontifical councils, and several other offices. The Secretariat of State, under the Cardinal Secretary of State, which is equivalent to a prime minister, directs and coordinates the Curia. Another important diplomatic role is played by the Secretary for Relations with States, which is equivalent to a Foreign Minister.

Since its formation as a sovereign entity, the Holy See has acted as a player on the world's diplomatic stage, not merely by moral statements, but also by entering into formal agreements and treaties with other states. According to the U.S. Department of State, the Holy See has diplomatic relations with the European Union (EU) in Brussels, and it is a permanent observer of the United Nations Organization (UN), Organization of American States (OAS) in Washington, African Union (AU), World Tourist Organization (WToO), World Trade Organization (WToO), World Health Organization (WHO), World Food Program (WFP), United Nations Educational, Scientific and Cultural Organization (UNESCO), United Nations Environment Program (UNEP), United Nations International Drug Control Program (UNDCP), United Nations Center for Human Settlements (UNCHS), Latin Union (LU), International Organization for Migration (IOM), International Labor Organization (ILO), International Fund for Agricultural Development (IFAD), and the United Nations Food and Agriculture Organization (FAO).[5]

Advocacy for the Environment

In recent years, the diplomatic involvements of the Holy See have increasingly included environmental concerns, in keeping with the intent of the Eighth Commandment for the Environment.

One important example occurred in May 2008, when Archbishop Celestino Migliore, the Holy See's permanent observer to the United Nations, issued a declaration attached to the Instrument of Accession to the Vienna Convention for the Protection of the Ozone Layer, to the Montreal Protocol on Substances that Deplete the Ozone Layer, and to its four amendments. At that time, the Holy See explained that it "desires to encourage the entire international community to be resolute in promoting authentic cooperation between politics, science, and economics. Such cooperation, as has been shown in the case of the ozone regime, can achieve important outcomes, which make it simultaneously possible to safeguard creation, to promote integral human development and to care for the common good, in a spirit of responsible solidarity and with profound positive repercussions for present and future generations."[6]

For Benedict, international legal protections come back to certain fundamentals—the recognition of the dignity of each individual, the unity of the human family, and the common good. As he said in his Message for the 2008 World Day of Peace, "Every man and woman [ought] to have a more lively sense of belonging to the one human family, and to strive to make human coexistence increasingly reflect this conviction, which is essential for the establishment of true and lasting peace."[7]

But it isn't enough for individuals to feel that sense of unity in the privacy of their own lives. For Benedict, a sense of unity and an appreciation for the common good must extend to the international level as well. As he told the Director General of the Food and Agriculture Organization:

> Today more than ever, in the face of recurring crises and the pursuit of narrow self-interest, there has to be cooperation and solidarity between states, each of which should be attentive to the needs of its weakest citizens, who are the first to suffer from poverty. Without this

solidarity, there is a risk of limiting or even impeding the work of international organizations that set out to fight hunger and malnutrition. In this way, they build up effectively the spirit of justice, harmony and peace among peoples: *"opus iustitiae pax"* (cf. Is 32:17).[8]

Promoting the Common Good

A detailed list of the international activities of the Holy See with regard to the environment, while impressive, is not as important as understanding what Pope Benedict believes can be accomplished through international efforts. The *Compendium* explains what the Vatican—and by extension Benedict himself—believes can happen when nations work together for the common good of the environment. These points include:

- ෨ Uniform rules will allow states to "exercise more effective control over the various activities that have negative effects on the environment and to protect ecosystems by preventing the risk of accidents."

- ෨ Individual states must "actively endeavor" within their own territories "to prevent destruction of the atmosphere and biosphere, by carefully monitoring, among other things, the impact of new technological or scientific advances . . . [and] ensuring that [their] citizens are not exposed to dangerous pollutants or toxic wastes."

- ෨ "The juridical content of the right to a safe and healthy natural environment is gradually taking form, stimulated by the concern shown by public opinion to disciplining the use of created goods according to the demands of the common good and a common desire to punish those who pollute." (*Compendium*, 468)

The idea of both human dignity and diplomatic relations focusing on the common good are themes Benedict consistently returns to. In late December 2008, while welcoming the new ambassador of Fiji to the Holy See, he stated:

> The Holy See's diplomatic relations with States can make an important contribution to the common good. While governments take responsibility for the political ordering of the State, the Church unceasingly proclaims her vision of the God-given dignity and rights of the human person. It is on this basis that she urges political leaders to ensure that all their people can live in peace and freedom, without fear of discrimination or injustice of any kind.[9]

But as much as juridical measures and diplomatic engagements are important, they are not enough to save the planet, Pope Benedict insists. Time and again, he asserts that governments—and even religious institutions—can do only so much. In the end, individuals must recognize and accept personal responsibility by making lasting changes in both mentality and lifestyle. As he said in a conference in Bolzano-Bressanone in August 2008, "We ourselves (must) find a new way of living, a discipline of making sacrifices, a discipline of the recognition of others to whom creation belongs as much as it belongs to us who may more easily make use of it."[10]

Or, as he reiterated in his Christmas message 2008, "If people look only to their own interests, our world will certainly fall apart."[11]

DISCIPLINE

IS NOT A

FOUR-LETTER WORD

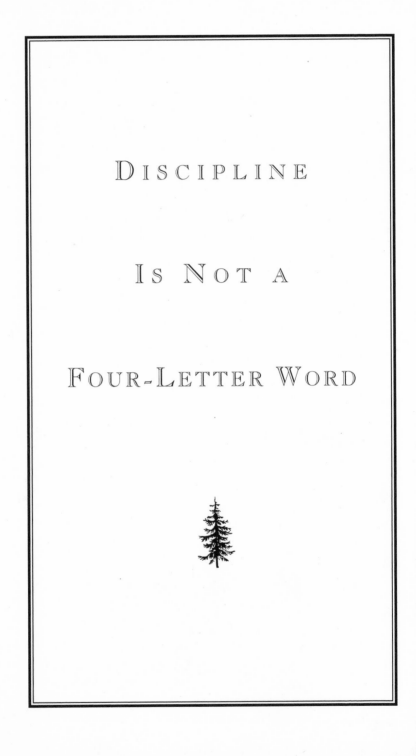

LIFESTYLES SHOULD BE ORIENTED ACCORD-
ING TO THE PRINCIPLES OF SOBRIETY, TEM-
PERANCE, AND SELF-DISCIPLINE, BOTH AT
THE PERSONAL AND SOCIAL LEVELS.
**PEOPLE NEED TO ESCAPE FROM THE
CONSUMER MENTALITY AND PROMOTE
METHODS OF PRODUCTION THAT
RESPECT THE CREATED ORDER, AS WELL
AS SATISFYING THE BASIC NEEDS OF ALL.**
THIS CHANGE OF LIFESTYLE WOULD BE
HELPED BY A GREATER AWARENESS OF THE
INTERDEPENDENCE THAT TIES TOGETHER
ALL THE INHABITANTS OF THE EARTH.

You don't have to be the proverbial rocket scientist, or even a scientist at all, to realize that we, as inhabitants of a planet in crisis, cannot continue to live the kind of lifestyle that we have been aspiring toward since the Industrial Revolution. As Pope Benedict observes in many of his messages, including his Epiphany 2009 speech, poisons and pollution in the world could destroy our present and our future[1] unless we rein in our unbridled consumption and consumerism and adopt lifestyles based on self-restraint and moderation.

Although many people around the world live simple lives, their simplicity is often the result of poverty and lack of opportunity, not conscious choice. The Western way of life, as much as it might be decried in some circles, is still widely envied. That's because, as the Ninth Commandment for the Environment points out, we are all intimately interconnected, sometimes in ways that we don't realize. Take for instance the proliferation and popularity of Hollywood movies and television shows. Even on the steppes of Mongolia, where people still maintain a semi-nomadic, herdsman way of life, solar generators and television sets can be seen at virtually every yurt.[2] What's being watched out there among the yaks and camels? Often Western movies and television shows that present lifestyles that were once limited to a handful of royalty but are now presented as something everyone can—and should—aspire to. It is no longer enough to have food, clothing, and shelter. We all want *foie gras*, Prada, and a mansion, preferably with a Porsche in the driveway—even when we live in an area that doesn't have paved roads.

Recent popes have all recognized that such flagrant emphasis on over-consumption cannot be sustained. In his 1967 encyclical *Populorum Progressio*, Pope Paul VI saw a fundamental link between consumerism and injustice, writing, "No one may appropriate surplus goods solely for his own private use when others lack the bare necessities of life. . . . The earth belongs to everyone, not to the rich" (par. 23). Pope John Paul II brought a spiritual emphasis to the discussion in *Centesimus Annus* when he criticized "a style of life which is presumed to be better when it is directed towards 'having' rather than 'being,'" while encouraging the creation of "lifestyles in which the quest for truth, beauty, goodness and communion with others for the sake of common growth are the factors which determine consumer choices, savings and investments" (par 36).

In some sense, Benedict's message is merely a continuation of the principles expressed by his predecessors, but what makes Benedict unique is that his views receive so much secular attention and approbation. As Gary Gardner, a senior researcher at the Worldwatch Institute, an environmental research organization based in Washington, D.C., writes, "Should Benedict raise the twin issues of consumption and population to the level of theological and spiritual attention they deserve, he would not only advance thinking on religious ethics, but also on how to create just and environmentally sustainable societies."[3]

Intriguingly, in the few short years of his pontificate, Benedict seems to have done just that. News outlets like FOX and others often carry pieces on his speeches that have environmental issues as part of their message. Benedict is seen as the "Green Pope" by people who have had only the dimmest awareness of what any Pope has had to say in the past.

The Holy See is aware of the opportunity to capitalize on this interest. Speaking to the U.N. in February 2008, Celestino Migliore addressed the entire world:

> Moreover, markets must be encouraged to patronize "green economics" and not to sustain demand for goods whose very production causes environmental degradation. Consumers must be aware that their consumption patterns have direct impact on the health of the environment. Thus through interdependence, solidarity and accountability, individuals and nations together will be more able to balance the needs of sustainable development with those of good stewardship at every level.[4]

But speeches are one thing. As this Commandment says, lifestyle is another. Saving the environment requires the latter even more than the former. Protecting the environment requires not only moderation and self-control, but a new way of thinking. On both a personal and social level it demands a break with the logic of consumerism.

Benedict himself has emphasized the way in which our lifestyles can be a form of *witness* to others. As he said in his question-and-answer session at the Diocese of Bolzano-Bressanone:

In fact, it's not just a question of finding techniques that can prevent environmental harms, even if it's important to find alternative sources of energy and so on. But all this won't be enough if we ourselves don't find a new style of life, a discipline which is made up in part of renunciations: a discipline of recognition of others, to whom creation belongs just as much as those of us who can make use of it more easily; a discipline of responsibility to the future for others and for ourselves. It's a question of responsibility before He who is our Judge, and as Judge our Redeemer, but nonetheless our Judge.

Therefore I think it's essential to hold together the two dimensions—Creation and Redemption, earthly life and eternal life, responsibility for creation and responsibility for others and for the future—and that it's our duty to intervene in a clear and decisive manner in public opinion. In order to be heard, we must at the same time demonstrate with our example, with our own style of life, that we are speaking of a message in which we ourselves believe, one by which it's possible to live. We want to ask the Lord to help us all live the faith, the responsibility of the faith, in such a way that our style of life becomes a form of witness, and that our words express the faith in a credible way as an orientation in our time.[5]

One of the more interesting ways that Benedict and the Holy See are encouraging lifestyle changes that serve both humanity and nature is through ecologically responsible tourism, not entirely surprising since the Vatican is a major tourist destination in itself. The Pontifical Council for Migrants and

Travelers for the 2008 World Tourism Day, as reported in Zenit, encouraged tourists to "contribute to keeping the planet alive and to curbing the gradual increase of alarming climate change" by cultivating "ethics of responsibility" and a "sense of limit against senseless development at all costs, fleeing from the obsession to possess and consume."

The pontifical council also gave some practical suggestions, including traveling more on foot, choosing hotels and hospitality centers that are ecologically conscious, taking less luggage on vehicles that use a lot of gas, planting trees, buying materials that are recyclable or biodegradable, favoring local arts and crafts, and respecting local legislation and the culture of the place visited. "It is possible to choose—there are still two paths before us—to be a tourist against the earth or in favor of it," stated the message. "This means that we are open to a consciousness of brotherhood on an earth that belongs to all and is for all, today and tomorrow."

To achieve this, the pontifical council suggested developing "a 'joyful austerity,' choosing that which is not transitory or corruptible. It is necessary to cultivate charity, also toward the earth, disarming the logic of death and strengthening that of love for this beloved space that belongs to us all . . . also for those who will come after us. . . . The great challenge is to overcome a certain insane narcissism, struggling against egoism and taking care, with lucidity and honesty, of an earth that runs the risk of being destroyed," it added. This means assuming "one's own responsibilities, at the individual and collective level, to recreate harmony." In conclusion, the council said, "It is not right that human beings bring about the end of the earth and the passing of generations through negligence or because of egoistic decisions and an exasperated consumerism, as if others and those who will come after us lacked value. In a word, there is an egoism regarding the future that is manifested in the absence of pondering and perspective, in indolence and abandonment."[6]

For all his encouragement to live a simpler lifestyle, Benedict is not recommending that everyone renounce all the good things of Creation. He himself is said to be fond of sweets, especially those from his home area of Bavaria. Adelholzener fruit nectar, Bavarian sausage from Franziskaner, his favorite restaurant, and buffalo mozzarella and potato ravioli with pancake strips are reported to be among his favorite foods.[7] For Benedict, it is not the enjoyment of the good things life has to offer that is the problem. It is the overemphasis on consumption that is an environmental sin. As always, Benedict's conviction is deeply rooted in his theological understanding of the role of nature and our relationship to it. As he wrote in *Values in a Time of Upheaval*:

> Nature resists unbridled consumption, and this is why the state of the environment has prompted new reflections on the direction that nature itself indicates. The lordship over nature of which the biblical creation narrative speaks does not mean a violent exploitation of nature, but rather an understanding of nature's inherent possibilities. This suggests a caution in the way in which we serve nature and natures serves us.[8]

Furthermore, as he said in *God and the World*:

> Man is indeed a kind of bridge. He is the point at which the material world and the spiritual world

meet and mingle and thus occupies a special place in the matrix of the created order. . . . That gives him a quite special function: that is to say, sharing the responsibility for the unity of creation, incarnating spirit in himself and, conversely, lifting material being up to God—and thereby, all in all, making a contribution to the great symphony of creation.[9]

Benedict understands that he is not in the business of giving people specifics as to how to reduce their consumption or to alter their lifestyles. His role is to encourage all of us, on international, national, and personal levels to examine our lives and the choices we make because we do occupy that "special place." In the end, however, Benedict's message actually is quite simple. In the words of St. Basil the Great:

The bread you do not use is the bread of the hungry.

The garment hanging in your wardrobe is the garment of the person who is naked.

The shoes you do not wear are the shoes of the one who is barefoot.

The money you keep locked away is the money of the poor.

The acts of charity you do not perform are the injustices you commit.

All Benedict might add is, "The planet you do not save is the earth you will not live upon."

It's All Gift

A SPIRITUAL RESPONSE MUST BE GIVEN TO ENVIRONMENTAL QUESTIONS, INSPIRED BY THE CONVICTION THAT CREATION IS A GIFT THAT GOD HAS PLACED IN THE HANDS OF MANKIND, TO BE USED RESPONSIBLY AND WITH LOVING CARE. PEOPLE'S FUNDAMENTAL ORIENTATION TOWARD THE CREATED WORLD SHOULD BE ONE OF GRATITUDE AND THANKFULNESS. THE WORLD, IN FACT, LEADS PEOPLE BACK TO THE MYSTERY OF GOD WHO HAS CREATED IT AND CONTINUES TO SUSTAIN IT. IF GOD IS FORGOTTEN, NATURE IS EMPTIED OF ITS DEEPEST MEANING AND LEFT IMPOVERISHED.

In the words of the poet T. S. Eliot, "What we call the beginning is often the end. And to make an end is to make a beginning." Thus, it is fitting that the last commandment for the environment should return us to Pope Benedict's primary vision and orientation toward creation.

For Benedict, there is really one thing to consider when it comes to environmental issues:

> What came first? Creative Reason, the Creator Spirit who makes all things and gives them growth, or Unreason, which, lacking any meaning, strangely enough brings forth a mathematically ordered cosmos, as well as man and his reason. The latter, however, would then be nothing more than a chance result of evolution and thus, in the end, equally meaningless. As Christians, we say: I believe in God the Father, the Creator of heaven and earth. I believe in the Creator Spirit. We believe that at the beginning of everything is the eternal Word, with Reason and not Unreason.[1]

Reason, with both a small and a capital "r," demands that we recognize that Creation is truly "a gift that God has placed in the hands of mankind, to be used responsibly and with loving care." As Benedict told the youth gathered in Loreto in the fall of 2007:

> The beauty of creation is one of the sources where we can truly touch God's beauty, we can see that the Creator exists and is good, which is

true as Sacred Scripture says in the Creation Narrative, that is, that God conceived of this world and made it with his heart, his will and his reason, and he found it good.[2]

Repeatedly, Benedict has stressed the absolute link between the goodness of Creation and the absolute goodness of its Creator. For instance, in his encyclical *Deus Caritas Est*, he wrote, "The universe in which we live has its source in God and was created by Him. . . . The whole world comes into existence by the power of his creative word. Consequently, his creation is dear to him, for it was willed by him and made by him" (par 9).

In *A New Song for the Lord* he explained, "We live in a world created by God along rational lines and he has entrusted this world to us so that we may rethink the thoughts of his reason with our reason and learn to govern, order and shape the world according to his thoughts."[3]

More than most, Benedict is keenly aware of the challenges of living a life of witness that holds Creation and Redemption together, blending both secular and spiritual considerations into a cohesive and comprehensible entity. As he told attendees at World Youth Day in Australia in 2008:

> The task of witness is not easy. There are many today who claim that God should be left on the sidelines, and that religion and faith, while fine for individuals, should either be excluded from the public forum altogether or included only in the pursuit of limited pragmatic goals. This secularist vision seeks to explain human life and shape society with little or no reference to the Creator. It presents itself as neutral, impartial and inclusive of everyone. But in reality, like

every ideology, secularism imposes a world-view. If God is irrelevant to public life, then society will be shaped in a godless image. When God is eclipsed, our ability to recognize the natural order, purpose, and the "good" begins to wane. What was ostensibly promoted as human ingenuity soon manifests itself as folly, greed and selfish exploitation. And so we have become more and more aware of our need for humility before the delicate complexity of God's world.[4]

As a concrete example of the type of witness Benedict is here describing, Benedict has related the following story from the life of the patron saint of the environment, that great lover of all creation, St. Francis of Assisi:

There is a story that goes as follows: Francis told the brother responsible for the garden never to plant the whole area with vegetables but to leave part of the garden for flowers, so that at every season of the year it may produce our sisters, the flowers, out of love for she who is called "the flower of the field and the lily of the valley" (Song 2:1). In the same way Francis wanted there always to be a particularly beautiful flower bed, so that, at all times, people would be moved by the sight of flowers to praise God. . . .

We cannot take this story and simply leave the religious element to one side as the relic of a bygone era, while appreciating its refusal of mean utility and its appreciation of the wealth of species. This would in no way correspond to what Francis did and intended. Above all, however, this story contains none of the bitterness that is directed against human beings (for their alleged interference in nature) such as one detects in so many conservationist manifestos today. When man himself is out of joint and can no longer affirm himself, nature cannot flourish. On the contrary: man must first be in harmony with himself; only then can he enter into harmony with creation and it with him. And this is only possible if he is in harmony with the Creator who designed both nature and us. Respect for man and respect for nature go together, but ultimately both can flourish and find their true measure only, if, in man and nature, we respect the Creator and his creation. The two only harmonize in relationship with the Creator. We shall assuredly never find the lost equilibrium if we refuse to press forward and discover this relationship. Let Francis of Assisi, then, make us reflect; let him set us on the right path.[5]

The words of Benedict and the commandments for the environment point the direction of the path we must take, but finally, it is up to us to shift our focus from what the earth can give us to a sense of gratitude that we have been given the earth in the first place.

In the end that is really the beginning, may we all join with Benedict in praying the "Canticle of the Sun," that great hymn of praise for nature written by St. Francis himself:

Most High, all-powerful, all-good Lord,
All praise is Yours, all glory, honor and blessings.
To you alone, Most High, do they belong;
no mortal lips are worthy to pronounce Your Name.

We praise You, Lord, for all Your creatures,
especially for Brother Sun,
who is the day through whom You give us light.
And he is beautiful and radiant with great splendor,
of You Most High, he bears your likeness.

We praise You, Lord, for Sister Moon and the stars,
in the heavens you have made them bright, precious
and fair.

We praise You, Lord, for Brothers Wind and Air,
fair and stormy, all weather's moods,
by which You cherish all that You have made.

We praise You, Lord, for Sister Water,
so useful, humble, precious and pure.

We praise You, Lord, for Brother Fire,
through whom You light the night.
He is beautiful, playful, robust, and strong.

We praise You, Lord, for Sister Earth,
who sustains us
with her fruits, colored flowers, and herbs.

We praise You, Lord, for those who pardon,
for love of You bear sickness and trial.
Blessed are those who endure in peace,
by You Most High, they will be crowned.

We praise You, Lord, for Sister Death,
from whom no-one living can escape.
Woe to those who die in their sins!
Blessed are those that She finds doing Your Will.
No second death can do them harm.

We praise and bless You, Lord, and give You thanks,
and serve You in all humility.

Notes

The Green Pope

1. Benedict XVI, "Mass for the Inauguration of the Pontificate of His Holiness Benedict XVI," April 24, 2005, http://www.vatican.va/ holy_father/benedict_xvi/homilies/2005/documents/ hf_ben-xvi_hom_20050424_inizio-pontificato_en.html.

2. Benedict XVI, "Homily of His Holiness Benedict XVI," Vienna, September 9, 2007, http://www.vatican.va/ holy_father/benedict_xvi/homilies/2007/documents/ hf_ben-xvi_hom_20070909_wien_en.html.

3. John L. Allen, "For a Favorite Diocese, Benedict Taps Leading Eco-theologian," *National Catholic Reporter Conversation Cafe*, December 5, 2008, http://ncrcafe.org/node/2315.

4. Benedict XVI, qtd. in Richard Owen, "Green Pope Urges Young People to Take Care of the Planet," *Times Online*, September 3, 2007, http://www.timesonline.co.uk/ tol/comment/faith/article2373715.ece.

5. Benedict XVI, "Message of His Holiness Benedict XVI to the Beloved People of Australia and to the Young Pilgrims Taking Part in World Youth Day 2008," July 4, 2008, http://www.vatican.va/holy_father/benedict_xvi/ messages/pont-messages/2008/documents/hf_ ben-xvi_mes_20080704_australia_en.html.

6. Benedict XVI, "Meeting with Priests, Deacons, and Seminarians of the Diocese of Bolzano-Bressanone," August 6, 2008, http://www.vatican.va/ holy_father/benedict_xvi/speeches/2008/august/ documents/hf_ben-xvi_spe_20080806_ clero-bressanone_en.html.

7. Ibid.

8. St. Francis of Assisi, "Canticle of the Sun." *The Writings of St. Francis of Assisi*, trans. Fr. Pascha Robinson (Philadelphia, PA: Dolphin Press, 1906).

9. St. Anthony of Padua, quoted in *The Wisdom of the Saints*, Jill Haak Adels (New York: Oxford University Press, 1987), 27.

10. John Paul II, "General Audience John Paul II," January 17, 2001, http://www.vatican.va/ holy_father/john_paul_ii/audiences/2001/documents/ hf_jp-ii_aud_20010117_en.html.

11. Philip Pullella, "Vatican Unveils Ambitious Solar Energy Plans," *Reuters*, November 26, 2008.

12. John Thavis, "Solar Panels on Vatican Hall First of Several Projects, Says Engineer," *Catholic News Service*, August 28, 2008, http://www.catholicnews.com/data/stories/cns/ 0804426.htm.

13. "Vatican Unveils."

COMMANDMENTS FOR THE ENVIRONMENT

1. U.S. Catholic Bishops, "Sharing Catholic Social Teaching: Challenges and Directions," http://www.usccb.org/ sdwp/projects/socialteaching/socialteaching.shtml.

2. John Paul II, "World Day of Peace 1990," January 1, 1990, http://www.vatican.va/holy_father/john_paul_ii/ messages/peace/documents/hf_jp-ii_mes_19891208_ xxiii-world-day-for-peace_en.html.

3. Pope John Paul II and Patriarch Bartholomew I, "Common Declaration on Environmental Ethics," June 6, 2002, http://www.vatican.va/holy_father/john_paul_ii/ speeches/2002/june/documents/hf_jp-ii_spe_20020610_ venice-declaration_en.html.

4. John L. Allen, "Interview with the Pope's New 'Eco-bishop,'" *National Catholic Reporter Conversation Cafe*, December 9, 2008, http://ncrcafe.org/node/2324

5. "Meeting with Priests, Deacons."

COMMANDMENT ONE

1. Lee Krystek, "Missing Mammoths," *The Museum of UnNatural Mystery*, http://www.unmuseum.org/ missingm.htm.

2. S.L. Vartanyan, "Radiocarbon Dating Evidence for Mammoths on Wrangel Island, Arctic Ocean, until 2000 BC." *Radiocarbon* 37, no. 1 (1995): 1–6. http://packrat.aml.arizona.edu/Journal/v37n1/ vartanyan.html.

3. M. A. Janssen and M. Scheffer, "Overexploitation of Renewable Resources by Ancient Societies and the Role of Sunk-Cost Effects," *Ecology and Society* 9, no. 1 (2004): 6, http://www.ecologyandsociety.org/vol9/iss1/art6.

4. Michael Lemonick, Hannah Block, Guy Garcia Palenque, Dos Pilas, and Laura Lopez. "Secrets of the Maya." *Time Magazine*, August 9, 1993, http://www.time.com/time/magazine/article/0,9171,979032-1,00.html.

5. "Historical Consequences of Deforestation: Easter Island," *Mongo Bay.Com*, http://www.mongabay.com/09easter_island.htm.

6. "Meeting with Priests, Deacons."

7. "Rainforest Facts," *RainTree.com*, http://www.raintree.com/facts.htm.

8. "Global Warming Statistics," *Effects of Global Warming*, http://www.effectofglobalwarming.com/global-warming-statistics.html.

9. Ibid.

10. Dan Joling, "Polar Bears May be Turning to Cannibalism," *Washingtonpost.com*, June 12, 2006, http://www.washingtonpost.com/wpdyn/content/article/2006/06/12/AR2006061201266.html.

11. "Great Apes Survival Partnership," *United Nations Environment Programme*, http://www.unep.org/grasp.

12. "Mass Extinction Underway," *The Well*, http://www.well.com/~davidu/extinction.html.

13. Benedict XVI, "Message of His Holiness," July 4, 2008.

14. Mark Maslin, *Global Warming: A Very Short Introduction* (New York: Oxford University Press, 2004), 10.

15. John Paul II, "General Audience," January 17, 2001, http://www.vatican.va/holy_father/john_paul_ii/audiences/2001/documents/hf_jp-ii_aud_20010117_en.html.

16. Benedict XVI, "Meeting of the Holy Father Benedict XVI with the Clergy of the Dioceses of Belluno-Feltre and Treviso, Church of St. Justin Martyr, Auronzo di Cadore," July 24, 2007, http://www.vatican.va/holy_father/benedict_xvi/speeches/2007/july/documents/hf_ben-xvi_spe_20070724_clero-cadore_en.html.

17. "Meeting with Priests, Deacons."

18. Cardinal Joseph Ratzinger, *"In the Beginning. . . ." A Catholic Understanding of the Story of Creation and the Fall*, trans. Boniface Ramsey, O.P. (Grand Rapids, MI: Wm. B. Eerdman's Publishing, 1995), 64.

19. John L. Allen, "Pope Strikes a Green Note on World Youth Day," *National Catholic Reporter*, July 25, 2008.

20. Cardinal Joseph Ratzinger, *God and the World: A Conversation With Peter Seewald*, trans. Henry Taylor (San Francisco: Ignatius Press, 2002), 78-79.

21. Benedict XVI, "Welcoming Celebration by the Young People, Address of His Holiness Benedict XVI," Barangaroo, Sydney Harbour, July 17, 2008, http://www.vatican.va/holy_father /benedict_xvi/speeches/2008/july/documents/ hf_ben-xvi_spe_20080717_barangaroo_en.html.

COMMANDMENT TWO

1. Nicholas Wade, *Before the Dawn* (New York: Penguin Press, 2006).

2. "Magisterium on Creation and Evolution," *ZENIT*, December 14, 2005, http://www.zenit.org/ article-14827?l = English.

3. Benedict XVI, "Address of His Holiness Benedict XVI to Members of the Pontifical Academy of Sciences on the Occasion of Their Plenary Assembly," October 31, 2008, http://www.vatican.va/holy_father/benedict_xvi/speeched /2008/october/documents/hf_ben-xvi_spe_20091031_ academy_sciences_en.html.

4. Cited in "Magisterium on Creation."

5. Benedict XVI, "Address to Members," October 31, 2008.

6. Cardinal Joseph Ratzinger, *Truth and Tolerance: Christian Belief and World Religions* (San Francisco: Ignatius Press, 2004), 182.

7. Ibid.

8. Ibid.

9. Cited in "Magisterium on Creation."

10. Benedict XVI, "Mass for the Inauguration," April 25, 2005.

COMMANDMENT THREE

1. Benedict XVI, "Message of His Holiness Pope Benedict XVI for the Celebration of the World Day of Peace," January 1, 2009, http://www.vatican.va/holy_father/benedict_xvi/messages/peace/documents/hf_ben-xvi_mes_20081208_xlii-world-day-peace_en.html.

2. R.A. Sturm, N.F. Box, and M. Ramsay, "Human Pigmentation Genetics," *NCBI Pub Med*, September 20, 1998, http://www.ncbi.nlm.nih.gov/pubmed/9819560.

3. Ian Fairlie and David Sumner, "The Other Report on Chernobyl," *The Greens: European Free Alliance*, http://www.greens-efa.org/cms/topics/dokbin/118/118499/the_other_report_on_chernobyl_torch@en.pdf.

4. Ibid.

5. Ibid.

6. Benedict XVI, "Angelus Address," Papal Summer Residence, Castel Gondolfo, September 16, 2007, http://www.vatican.va/holy_father/benedict_xvi/angelus/2007/documents/hf_ben-xvi_ang_20070916_en.html.

7. Celestino Migliore, "Intervention by the Holy See at the Second Committee of the 63rd Session of the UN General Assembly on Sustainable Development," October 10, 2008, http://www.vatican.va/roman_curia/secretariat_state/2008/documents/rc_seg-st_20081028_sustainable-development_en.html.

8. John Paul II, "Apostolic Letter *Dilecti Amici* of Pope John Paul II to the Youth of the World on the Occasion of International Youth Year," March 31, 1985, http://www.vatican.va/holy_father/john_paul_ii/apost_letters/documents/hf_jp-ii_apl_31031985_dilecti-amici_en.html.

9. "Pope Strikes."

10. Ibid.

11. Benedict XVI, "Welcoming Celebration," July 17, 2008.

12. Benedict XVI, "Message of His Holiness," July 4, 2008.

13. Ibid.

14. Benedict XVI, "Welcoming Celebration," July 17, 2008.

15. Ibid.

16. Ibid.

17. Benedict XVI, "Homily of His Holiness Benedict XVI," September 2, 2007, http://www.vatican.va/holy_father/benedict_xvi/homilies/2007/documents/hf_ben-xvi_hom_20070 902_loreto_en.html.

18. Benedict XVI, "Message for the Celebration of the World Day of Peace 2007," January 1, 2007, http://www.vatican.va/holy_father/benedict_xvi/messages/peace/documents/hf_ben-xvi_mes_20061208_xl-world-day-peace_en.html.

19. Benedict XVI, "Welcoming Celebration," July 17, 2008.

20. Cardinal Joseph Ratzinger, *"In the Beginning. . . ."*, 100.

COMMANDMENT FOUR

1. Benedict XVI, "Address on the Occasion of the Plenary Assembly of the Pontifical Council for Health Pastoral Care," March 22, 2007, http://www.vatican.va/holy_father/benedict_xvi/speeches/2007/march/documents/hf_ben-xvi_spe_20070322_pc-salute_en.html.

2. Benedict XVI, "60th anniversary of the Italian Christian Workers' Associations," January 27, 2006, http://www.vatican.va/holy_father/benedict_xvi/speeches/2006/january/documents/hf_benxvi_spe_20060127_acli_en.html.

3. Benedict XVI, *Values in a Time of Upheaval* (San Francisco: Ignatius Press, 2006), 25.

4. Gwynne Lyons, "Effects of Pollutants on the Reproductive Health of Male Vertebrate Wildlife—Males Under Threat," *ChemTrust,* http://www.chemtrust.org.uk/documents/Male%20Wildlife%20Under%20Threat%202008%20full%20report.pdf.

5. "Genetically Modified Foods and Organisms," *Human Genome Project Information,* http://www.ornl.gov/sci/techresources/Human_Genome/elsi/gmfood.shtml.

6. John Pope, "Glow-in-the-Dark Cat a Genetic Success," *Ajcpets*, October 22, 2008, http://www.ajc.com/services/content/pets/stories/2008/10/22/glowing_cat_green_genes.html.
   An orange tabby, the result of a genetic experiment at the Audubon Center for Research of Endangered Species, has eyes, gums, and tongue that glow a vivid lime green under ultraviolet light.

7. "Genetically Modified Foods."

8. "Transgenic Pollen Harms Monarch Larvae." *Nature* 399, no. 6733 (May 1999): 214.

9. "Iranian scientist creates sheep with half-human organs," *PressTV*, http://www.presstv.ir/detail.aspx?id=3995&sectionid=3510208.

10. Cardinal Rigali's statement is available at the USCCB website: http://www.usccb.org/comm/archives/2008/08-062.shtml.

11. Cardinal Joseph Ratzinger, *"In the Beginning. . . . "*, 37.

12. Benedict XVI and Patriarch Batholomew I, "Common Declaration by His Holiness Benedict XVI and Patriarch Bartholomew I," November 30, 2006, http://www.vatican.va/holy_father/benedict_xvi/speeches/2006/november/documents/hf_ben-xvi_spe_20061130_dichiarazione-comune_en.html.

COMMANDMENT FIVE

1. P.H. Liotta and Allan W. Shearer, *Gaia's Revenge: Climate Change and Humanity's Loss* (Westport, CT: Praeger Publishers, 2007), 2.

2. James Lovelock, *The Ages of Gaia* (New York: W.W. Norton, 1995), 27.

3. "Divinization of Nature as Ecological Sin," *ZENIT*, March 9, 2005, http://www.zenit.org/article-12464?l=english.

4. Benedict XVI, "Message for the celebration of the World Day of Peace 2007," January 1,2007, http://www.vatican.va/holy_father/benedict_xvi/messages/peace/documents/hf_ben-xvi_mes_20061208_xl-world-day-peace_en.html.

5. Benedict XVI, "Message for the Celebration of the World Day of Peace 2008," January 1, 2008, http://www.vatican.va/holy_father/benedict_xvi/messages/peace/documents/hf_ben-xvi_mes_20071208_xli-world-day-peace_en.html.

6. "A Christian View of Man and Nature," *ZENIT*, November 12, 2005, http://www.zenit.org/article-17658?l=english.

7. Ibid.

8. Ibid.

9. "Great Wall Across the Yangtze, Three Gorges Dam—Facts and Figures," *PBS*, http://www.pbs.org/itvs/greatwall/dam1.html.

10. Ibid.

11. Anthony Barich and Catherine Smibert, "3-Minute Showers and Lots of Walking," *ZENIT*, July 15, 2008, http://www.zenit.org/article-23212?l=english.

Commandment Six

1. "Intervention by the Holy See."

2. "The Exxon Valdez Oil Spill Disaster," *ExploreNorth*, March 24, 1999, http://explorenorth.com/library/weekly/aa032499.htm.

3. "Cost of Cutting Carbon: Pennies a Day—Global Warming," *Environmental Defense Fund*, March 11, 2008, http://www.edf.org/article.cfm?contentID=5405.

4. Benedict XVI, "Letter of His Holiness Benedict XVI to the Ecumenical Patriarch of Constantinople on the Occasion of the Seventh Symposium of the Religion, Science, and the Environment Movement," September 1, 2007, http://www.vatican.va/holy_father/benedict_xvi/letters/2007/documents/hf_ben-xvi_let_20070901_symposium-environment_en.html.

5. Benedict XVI, "Message du Pape Benoît XVI Signé par L'archevêque Fernando Filoni, Substitut de la Secrétairerie D'etat, à L'occasion de la 82 Édition des Semaines Sociales de France," November 21, 2007, translated by the author, http://www.vatican.va/roman_curia/secretariat_state/2007/documents/rc_segst_20071121_settimane-francia_fr.html.

6. Benedict XVI, "Letter . . . to the Ecumenical Patriarch," September 1, 2007.

7. Msgr. Renato R. Martino,"World Summit on Sustainable Development," September 2, 2002, http://www.vatican.va/roman_curia/secretariat_state/documents/rc_seg-st_doc_20020902_martino-johannesburg_en.html.

8. Msgr. Celestino Migliore, "Intervention by the Holy See at the 15th Session of the Commission on Sustainable Development of the United Nations Economic and Social Council," May 10, 2007, http://www.vatican.va/roman_curia/secretariat_state/2007/documents/rc_seg-st_20070510_ecosoc_en.html.

9. Amir Taheri, "For How Long Will Oil Reserves Last?" *Alarabiya News Channel*, November 7, 2007, http://www.alarabiya.net/views/2007/11/07/41357.html.

10. Elaine Frey, "Tropical Deforestation in the Amazon: An Economic Analysis of Rondonia, Brazil." *Political Economy,* 11 (2002).

11. Benedict XVI, "Message to the Director General of the Food and Agriculture Organization (FAO)," October 16, 2006, http://www.vatican.va/holy_father/benedict_xvi/ messages/food/documents/hf_ben-xvi_mes_20061016_ world-food-day-2006_en.html.

12. "Intervention by the Holy See," October 28, 2008.

13. Benedict XVI, "Address of His Holiness Benedict XVI to H.E. Mr. Isaac Chikwekwere Lamba, New Ambassador of the Republic of Malawi to the Holy See," December 18, 2008, http://www.vatican.va/holy_father/benedict_xvi/ speeches/2008/december/documents/hf_ben-xvi_spe_ 20081218_malawi_en.html

COMMANDMENT SEVEN

1. Benedict XVI, "Message . . . for the Celebration of the World Day of Peace," January 1, 2009, http://www.vatican.va/ holy_father/benedict_xvi/messages/peace/documents/ hf_ben-xvi_mes_20081208_xlii-world-day-peace_en.html

2. Benedict XVI, "Message du Pape Benoît XVI."

3. Benedict XVI, "Address to the New Ambassadors Accredited to the Holy See," June 16, 2005, http://www.vatican.va/ holy_father/benedict_xvi/speeches/2005/june/ documents/hf_benxvi_spe_20050616_ambassadors_en.html.

4. Philip Emeagwali, "Technology Widens Rich-Poor Gap," *The Perspective,* October 8, 2007, http://www.liberiaitech.com/ theperspective/2007/1007200702.html.

5. "Water, An Essential Element for Life: A Contribution of the Holy See to the Fourth World Water Forum, An Update," March 16, 2006, http://www.vatican.va/roman_curia/ pontifical_councils/justpeace/documents/ rc_pc_justpeace_doc_20060322_mexico-water_en.html.

6. Ibid.

7. John Thavis, "Scientists, ethicists say water is essential resource of the future," *Catholic News Service,* November 15, 2005, http://www.catholicnews.com/data/stories/cns/ 0506530.htm.

8. "Water, An Essential Element for Life: March 16, 2006.

9. Renato R. Martino, "A Contribution of the Delegation of the Holy See on the Occasion of the Third World Water Forum," March 16, 2003, http://www.vatican.va/roman_curia/pontifical_councils/justpeace/documents/rc_pc_justpeace_doc_20030322_kyoto-water_en.html.

10. Benedict XVI, "Eucharistic Celebration in the Cathedral of the Holy Spirit of Istanbul," December 1, 2006, http://www.vatican.va/holy_father/benedict_xvi/homlies/2006/documents/hf_ben-xvi_hom_20061201_istanbul_en.html.

11. "Beyond Scarcity: Power, Poverty and the Global Water Crisis," *Human Development Reports,* 6, 7, 35, http://hdr.undp.org/en/reports/global/hdr2006.

12. "Childhood Under Threat," *UNICEF,* http://www.unicef.org/sowc05/english/index.html.

13. Maude Barlow, "Water as Commodity—The Wrong Prescription." *The Institute for Food and Development Policy* 7 no. 3 (2001).

14. "Capital lacks clean water, cholera kills hundreds in Zimbabwe," *CNN.com,* December 1, 2008, http://www.cnn.com/2008/WORLD/africa/12/01/zimbabwe.cholera/index.html?iref=mpstoryview.

15. Abid Aslam, "Bottled Water: Nectar of the Frauds?" *Common Dreams News Center,* February 5, 2006, http://www.commondreams.org/headlines06/0205-01.htm.

16. Benedict XVI, "Message . . . for the Celebration of the World Day of Peace," December 8, 2008.

COMMANDMENT EIGHT

1. Carol Glatz, "World's Busiest Pharmacy? Vatican Drugstore Offers Cut-Rate Prices," *Catholic News Service,* May 23, 2008, http://www.catholicnews.com/data/stories/cns/0802820.htm.

2. Bureau of European and Eurasian Affairs, "Background Note: The Holy See," *U.S. Department of State,* December 2008, http://www.state.gov/r/pa/ei/bgn/3819.htm.

3. Ibid.

4. Ibid.

5. Ibid. The Vatican is also an observer on an informal basis of the World Meteorological Organization in Geneva (WMO), United

Nations Committee of Peaceful Use of Outer Space (UNCOPU-OS), International Strategy for Disaster Reduction (ISDR), International Maritime Organization (IMO), African Asian Legal Consultative Committee (AALCC), and the International Civil Aviation Organization (ICAO), as well as being s a member of the Organization for the Prohibition of Chemical Weapons (OPCW), Organization for Security and Cooperation in Europe (OSCE), International Telecommunication Union (ITU), International Telecommunication Satellite Organization (ITSO), World Intellectual Property Organization (WIPO), Universal Postal Union (UPU), International Institute for the Unification of Private Law (UNIDROIT), United Nations High Commissioner for Refugees (UNHCR), United Nations Conference on Trade and Development (UNCTAD), International Grains Council (IGC), International Committee for Military Medicine (ICMM), International Atomic Energy Agency (IAEA), and the Preparatory Commission for the Comprehensive Nuclear Test Ban Treaty Organization (CTBTO), and the Bureau of European and Eurasian Affairs.

6. "Holy See's Commitment to Protecting Ozone Layer," *ZENIT*, May 6, 2008, http://www.zenit.org/article -22510?l = english.

7. Benedict XVI, "Message . . . for the Celebration of the World Day of Peace," January 1, 2008.

8. Benedict XVI, "Message to the Director General of the Food and Agriculture Organization," October 16, 2006, http://www.vatican.va/holy_father/benedict_xvi/ messages/food/documents/hf_ben-xvi_mes_20061016_ world-food-day-2006_en.html.

9. Benedict XVI, "To the New Ambassador of the Republic of the Fiji Islands to the Holy See," December 18, 2008, http://www.vatican.va/holy_father/benedict_xvi/ speeches/2008/december/index_en.htm.

10. Benedict XVI, "Meeting with Priests, Deacons."

11. Benedict XVI, "*Urbi et Orbi* Message of His Holiness Pope Benedict XVI," Christmas 2008, http://www.vatican.va/ holy_father/benedict_xvi/messages/urbi/documents/ hf_ben-xvi_mes_20081225_urbi_en.html

Commandment Nine

1. Benedict XVI, "Homily," January 6, 2009. http://www. vatican.va/holy_father/benedict_xvi/homilies/2009/ documents/hf_ben-xvi_hom_20090106_epifania_en.html

2. Alyce Dengler, Ph.D. (Norman, OK: Department of Anthropology, University of Oklahoma, October 2007), personal interview.

3. Gary Gardner, *Inspiring Progress: Religions' Contributions to Sustainable Development* (New York: W.W. Norton, 2006).

4. Celestino Migliore, "Addressing Climate Change: the United Nations and the World at Work," February 12, 2008, http://www.vatican.va/roman_curia/secretariat_state/2008 /documents/rc_seg-st_20080212_climate-change_en.html.

5. Benedict XVI, "Meeting with Priests, Deacons."

6. "Vatican Urges Earth-Friendly Vacations," *ZENIT,* June 16, 2008. http://www.zenit.org/article-23024?l=english.

7. "Pope Benedict XVI," *Cultural Catholic,* http://www.cultural catholic.com/PopeBenedictXVI.htm.

8. Benedict XVI, *Values in a Time,* 159.

9. Joseph Cardinal Ratzinger, *God and the World,* 89.

Commandment Ten

1. Stephen Otto Horn and Siegfried Wiedenhofer, editors, *Creation and Evolution: A Conference with Pope Benedict XVI in Castel Gandolfo* (San Francisco: Ignatius Press, 2007).

2. Benedict XVI, "Pastoral Visit of His Holiness Benedict XVI to Loreto on the Occasion of the Agora of Italian Youth," September 1, 2007, http://www.vatican.va/holy_father/ benedict_xvi/speeches/2007/september/documents/hf_be n-xvi_spe_20070901_veglia-loreto_en.html#Address_of_his_ Holiness_Benedict_XVI.

3. Benedict XVI, *A New Song for the Lord* (New York: Crossroad Publishing, 2005).

4. Benedict XVI, "Message of His Holiness," July 4, 2008.

5. Cardinal Joseph Ratzinger, *Seek That Which is Above: Meditations Through the Year*. Trans. Graham Harrison (San Francisco: Ignatius Press, 2007), 176.

WOODEENE KOENIG-BRICKER is the former editor of *Catholic Parent* magazine
and a journalist who has written
extensively about spirituality and family for magazines such as *McCall's,
Family Circle, Working Parents,
Marriage and Family, Catholic Digest,*
and *Our Sunday Visitor.* She is also the
author of several books, including *365
Saints: Your Daily Guide to the Wisdom
and Wonder of Their Lives* and *Asking
God for the Gifts He Wants to Give You.*

Founded in 1865, Ave Maria Press,
a ministry of the Congregation of
Holy Cross, is a Catholic publishing
company that serves the spiritual and
formative needs of the Church and its
schools, institutions, and ministers;
Christian individuals and families; and
others seeking spiritual nourishment.

For a complete listing of titles from

Ave Maria Press

Sorin Books

Forest of Peace

Christian Classics

visit www.avemariapress.com

ave maria press / Notre Dame, IN 46556
A Ministry of the Indiana Province of Holy Cross